CONTENTS

بِسْمِ اللَّهِ الرَّحْمَٰنِ الرَّحِيمِ

NABUWWA (PROPHETHOOD)

According to Islamic terminology the word nabi means one who is sent by Allah to guide us. A rasul is one who is sent by Allah and brings a new shari'a (Laws of living).

In the English language both nabi (pl. Ambiya) and rasul (pl. Mursaleen) are referred to as Prophets.

Allah sent 124,000 Prophets to guide us. The first of them was Prophet Adam (pbuh) and the last one was Prophet Muhammad (pbuh)

Many of the Prophets were sent to one or two villages, some even to one family.

Others were sent to a bigger area or to one tribe. But none of them were sent for the whole of mankind like our Prophet Muhammad (pbuh).

Five of these Prophets are known as Ulul Adhm Prophets (those given a great responsibility). They are:

1.   Prophet Nuh (pbuh)
2.   Prophet Ibraheem (pbuh)
3.   Prophet Musa (pbuh)
4.   Prophet Isa (pbuh)
5.   Prophet Muhammad (pbuh)

Allah sent down words to guide us. These words were written down into books. There were many books.

The four important ones are:
*   Zabur given to Prophet Dawud (pbuh)
*   Tawraat given to Prophet Musa (pbuh)
*   Injeel given to Prophet Isa (pbuh)
*   Qur'an given to Prophet Muhammad (pbuh)

وَقُل رَّبِّ زِدْنِي عِلْمًا

PROPHETS MENTIONED IN QUR'AN & AHADITH

1. Adam (pbuh)	15. Harun (pbuh)
2. Idrees (pbuh)	16. Ilyaas (pbuh)
3. Nuh (pbuh)	17. Ilyasa (pbuh)
4. Hud (pbuh)	18. Dhul-Kifl (pbuh)
5. Saalih (pbuh)	19. Dhul-Qarnain (pbuh)
6. Ibrahim (pbuh)	20. Uzayr (pbuh)
7. Lut (pbuh)	21. Dawud (pbuh)
8. Ismail (pbuh)	22. Sulayman (pbuh)
9. Is-haaq (pbuh)	23. Luqman (pbuh)*
10. Ya'qub (pbuh)	24. Yunus (pbuh)
11. Yusuf (pbuh)	25. Zakariyya (pbuh)
12. Ayyub (pbuh)	26. Yahya (pbuh)
13. Shuayb (pbuh)	27. Isa (pbuh)
14. Musa (pbuh)	28. Muhammad (pbuh)

*He was an Ethiopian wise man - Majority of Muslims believe he was a Prophet.

Who is a Prophet?

A Prophet must be the perfect person in his time in everything like knowledge, akhlaq, taqwa, bravery......

He must also have the following qualifications:

1. He must be sent by Allah. A Prophet cannot be chosen by the people.

2. He must have 'isma. This means that he must not do anything to displease Allah even by mistake. A Prophet therefore does not commit anysins.

3. He must be able to perform miracles- Mu'jiza. A miracle is something that nobody else can do. Miracles are performed by permission of and power given by Allah.

The miracles of Prophet Musa (pbuh) are that hi staff turned into a snake whenever he threw it down and his hand shone like a lamp every time he placed it under his armpit and took it out. The miracles of Prophet Isa (pbuh) are that he could cure the sick and bring the dead back to life.

The miracle of our Prophet Muhammad (pbuh) is the Qur'an.

PROPHET ADAM (PBUH)

NAME: Prophet Adam(pbuh)

TITLE: (Chosen one ofAllah).

                   Khalifatullah (1st Deputy of Allah).

CHILDREN: Habil, Kabil, Sheeth and others.

Allah created Prophet Adam (pbuh) from clay and then blew his spirit into the clay form. He taught Prophet Adam (pbuh) all the names i.e. knowledge, speech, expression etc.

He then commanded all the angels to do sajda (prostrate) before Prophet Adam (pbuh). They all obeyed except Shaytan (he was a jinn who lived amongst the angels). Shaytan did not prostrate because he said he was better than Prophet Adam (pbuh) as he was made from fire and Prophet Adam (pbuh) was made from clay. He was sent out of heaven but was allowed respite (leave from punishment) until a day chosen by Allah. Allah then asked Prophet Adam (pbuh) and his wife Hawwa (pbuh) to live in the garden of paradise. They were allowed to eat of all the fruits but were advised not to go near one particular tree and not to eat of its fruits.

Shaytan was always angry at Prophet Adam (pbuh) at being the cause of his being sent out of heaven so he entered paradise and told Prophet Adam (pbuh) that he was their friend and was advising them. He told them to eat of the fruit they were asked not to go near because besides being tasty it would make them be like angels and live forever. Adam and Hawwa were tricked and tasted the fruit. As soon as they did they realised their mistake and turned to Allah for forgiveness. He forgave them but asked them to leave paradise and to go and live on the earth where as long as they obeyed Allah, Shaytan would not be able to trick them.

It is related that when Prophet Adam (pbuh) was sent to the earth they first arrived at a place called Arafa. Here on the mountain called Jabal ur Rahma, he cried for forgiveness of his mistake. Allah forgave him. From Arafa Prophet Adam (pbuh) and Hawwa (pbuh) went through Muzdalifa and Mina to Makka. To complete his forgiveness Allah asked Prophet Adam (pbuh) to do a tawaf round where the Ka'ba was going to be. Jibrail drew a square showing him where the Ka'ba was to be and Prophet Adam (pbuh) did tawaf.

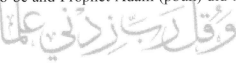

Hawwa (pbuh) was asked to go away from Adam's sight and told to sit on the mountain of Marwa. On completion of his tawaf Prophet Adam (pbuh) looked for Hawwa (pbuh). He climbed the nearest mountain to the Ka'ba which was Mount Safa and saw his wife on the opposite mountain. He went towards her but before meeting her he was asked by Allah to cut his nails and hair which he had not looked after and let grow due to his grief committing a mistake. He did this and on meeting Hawwa (pbuh) he was asked to perform another tawaf (Tawaf-un-Nisa) in thanks. This was the first Umraperformed.

PROPHET ADAM (PBUH)
Achoo!

Prophet Adam (pbuh) was the first human being created by Allah. Allah asked the angels to bring different types of clay from the earth.

The clay was then mixed with water and left for a while (like bread dough). He then shaped it into the form of a man and left it to set.

When it was strong He made the man come alive and it was Prophet Adam (pbuh) As soon as he was alive Prophet Adam (pbuh)sneezed.

As soon as he had sneezed he said:

Alhamdulillah

(All praise is for Allah)

PROPHET ADAM (PBUH)
"No! I will not do sajda."

After Allah had made Prophet Adam (pbuh) He called all the angels and asked them to do sajda to Prophet Adam (pbuh)

Shaytan (Iblees) was there as well and was asked to do the same. All the angels obeyed Allah and did sajda but Shaytan refused! When he was asked why he had refused he said he was better than Prophet Adam (pbuh) because he was made of fire and Prophet Adam (pbuh) was made of clay.

Shaytan was only looking at the outside of Prophet Adam (pbuh) and not his inside (nafs).

Allah was very angry that Shaytan disobeyed Him. He sent Shaytan away from the heavens.

Ever since then Shaytan has tried to make people disobey Allah. He succeeds when our faith in Allah is not strong.

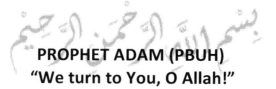

PROPHET ADAM (PBUH)
"We turn to You, O Allah!"

Allah asked Prophet Adam (pbuh) and his wife Sayyida Hawwa (pbuh) to live in Janna.

They were allowed to eat whatever they wanted but they were advised not to go near one tree.

Shaytan got jealous and he went to visit Prophet Adam (pbuh) and Sayyida Hawwa (pbuh) in Janna pretending to be a wise man. He told them that if they ate the fruit of the tree which they were not supposed to go near, they would become angels and will never die.

As soon as they ate the fruit of the tree they realised that they had been tricked by Shaytan. They turned to Allah and said sorry asking Him to forgivethem.

Allah forgave them but they were asked to leave Janna and were sent down to the earth.

HABIL & QABIL (CANE & ABEL)

Prophet Adam (pbuh) and Hawwa (pbuh) had two sons whose names were Habil and Qabil. Allah sent wives for them from heaven.

Habil was a herdsman and Qabil was a farmer.

When Prophet Adam (pbuh) chose Habil to be his successor Qabil got very angry and jealous, so Prophet Adam (pbuh) told them to offer a sacrifice to Allah and the one whose sacrifice was accepted would be his successor.

Habil offered the best of his flock whilst Qabil brought some withered ears of corn. Allah accepted Habil's sacrifice.

Qabil in his jealousy killed his brother. He did not know what to do with Habil's body. Allah sent a crow to show Qabil how to bury his brother's body.

Qabil settled with his family in the east of Eden and was a fire worshipper. He and his family were all drowned in the flood of Nuh (pbuh).

Prophet Adam (pbuh) was very shocked and cried for a long time at the murder of Habil (pbuh). Allah then granted him a son called Sheeth (pbuh).

وَقُل رَّبِّ زِدْنِي عِلْمَاً

THE SONS OF PROPHET ADAM (PBUH)
"I will not stretch out my hand to kill you."

Prophet Adam (pbuh) had two sons. One was called Habil and the other was called Qabil.

Habil was a good son and Prophet Adam (pbuh) chose him to be his successor. Qabil did not like that and argued with his father. Prophet Adam (pbuh) asked them both to offer a sacrifice to Allah. Whoever's sacrifice is accepted would be his successor.

Habil used to look after sheep and brought his best sheep as a sacrifice whilst Qabil, who was a farmer only brought some withered ears of corn.

Allah accepted the sacrifice of Habil.

Qabil was so jealous of his brother that he said to him:
"I will certainly kill you!"

Habil replied:
"If you stretch out your hand to kill me, I will not stretch out my hand to kill you, because I fear Allah, the Lord of the worlds!"

Qabil killed Habil but did not know what to do with his brother's body.

Allah sent two crows to show him. One killed the other and then buried the dead body. Qabil learnt what to do from the crows and buried his brother's body.

بِسْمِ اللَّهِ الرَّحْمَٰنِ الرَّحِيمِ

PROPHET SHEETH (PBUH) (SETH)

Prophet Sheeth (pbuh) was born five years after the death of Habil. Allah appointed Prophet Sheeth (pbuh) as the successor to Prophet Adam (pbuh), and sent him fifty books containing guidelines, commands, practices and restrictions. He was a virtuous son and it was he who buried Adam (pbuh) when he died.

It is related from Imam Ja'fer As-Sadiq (pbuh) that Sheeth (pbuh) led the funeral prayers for Prophet Adam (pbuh) and recited five Takbeers (a practise that we still perform today in Salaat-ul-Mayyit).

Prophet Sheeth (pbuh) resided in Makka, where he constantly performed Hajj. He died at the age of 912 years, leaving a successor. He was buried alongside his parents.

وَقُل رَّبِّ زِدْنِي عِلْمًا

IDREES (PBUH) (ENOCH)

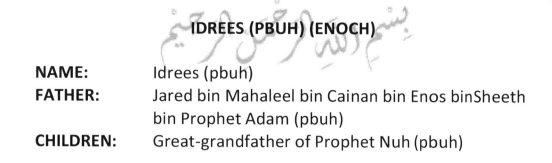

NAME: Idrees (pbuh)

FATHER: Jared bin Mahaleel bin Cainan bin Enos binSheeth bin Prophet Adam (pbuh)

CHILDREN: Great-grandfather of Prophet Nuh (pbuh)

Prophet Idrees (pbuh) was born 100 years after the death of Prophet Adam (pbuh).

He was the great grandson of Prophet Sheeth (pbuh) and the great great grandfather of Prophet Nuh (pbuh). He was the first person to introduce the art of writing and the art of tailoring (stitching). He was the first man also to make weapons and explain the measuring of weights by balance. It was he who taught people the wonders of the planets in relation to the sun and instructed them to worship the creator (Allah). It is related from Imam Ja'fer Sadiq (pbuh) that Prophet Idrees (pbuh) used to sit in the mosque of Sahla (in Kufa) and stitch and offer his prayers there.

It is narrated that during the Prophethood of Prophet Idrees (pbuh) there was once a cruel King. One day the King on an outing saw a beautiful garden which he liked. He asked the owner of the garden to hand over the garden to him. The owner refused saying he had a wife and children to feed. The king was enraged. His wife was also a mean woman, told him to ask some people to bear witness that the man was against the king and to then kill him.

The king did just that and took the land leaving the family of the garden owner
homeless.

Allah sent Prophet Idrees (pbuh) to warn the king of punishment for his crime. The King did not listen and told Prophet Idrees (pbuh) to leave before he was killed. The Queen sent some men to kill Idrees (pbuh). He left and hid in a cave praying to Allah to punish the people. The King was overthrown and the people of the town also suffered for there was no rain. Some 20 years later the people, through suffering, prayed to Allah for forgiveness. Allah accepted their repentance and rain was sent. Prophet Idrees (pbuh) returned to the town.

بِسْمِ اللَّهِ الرَّحْمَنِ الرَّحِيمِ

He used to pray so much that even the angels used to wonder about him. Once the angel of death Izrail wanted to visit Idrees (pbuh). Allah allowed him to do so in human form. Idrees (pbuh) asked Izrail to take his soul out as he wanted to taste death. Izrail did this but then returned his soul back. He then asked to see Janna and Jahannam. When he saw Janna, he asked to stay there for a while. Allah allowed him to do so as he had already tasted death. He is still alive and in heavens.

وَقُل رَّبِّ زِدْنِي عِلْمًا

PROPHET NUH (PBUH) (NOAH)

NAME: Abdul Ghaffar or Abdul Malek or AbdulA'laa

TITLE: Nuh (one who cries a lot - in
fear of Allah) Adam E Thaani
(2nd Adam)

CHILDREN: Haam, Saam, Yaafis, Kan'aan

He was born 126 years after the death of Prophet Adam (pbuh) and it is related that there were 10 Prophets before him and after Prophet Adam(pbuh).

Prophet Nuh (pbuh) preached and lived amongst his people for 950 years. His life span is mentioned by some to be 2500 years

He preached to his people about the oneness of Allah and asked them not to worship other gods but the chiefs and the people just ignored him, mocked at him and even beat him up. At times Prophet Nuh (pbuh) was buried under piles of stones and Jibrail used to come and remove the stones and tend the wounds.

The people then decided to leave him alone saying he was mad **(Qur'an 23:25)**.

Prophet Nuh (pbuh) after many years of preaching to no avail complained to Allah saying that although he called them night and day they were getting worse and would not listen putting their finger in their ears covering their faces so he could not see them nor could they hear him.

Allah stopped rain to them for 40-70 years but the people were so stubborn that they refused to believe and listen (Allah stopped granting them children too).

Allah asked Prophet Nuh (pbuh) to build an ark as he was going to see his punishment in the form of a flood.

When the people saw him and the believers making an ark they started laughing at him. The ark was made at a place which is now known as Masjid-e-Kufa. It was 1200 yds in length, 800 yds in width and 80 yds in height. It had three stories - the 1st for the animals, the 2nd for the birds and the 3rd for the 30 believers inclusive of Prophet Nuh (pbuh) and his family. When the ark was ready Allah asked Prophet Nuh (pbuh), his three sons, Haam, Saam and Yaafis, 72 believers and a pair of each kind of animal and bird to board the ark.

Prophet Nuh (pbuh) had another son called Kan'aan who refused to board the ark and was not a believer.

When they had all boarded the ark they were asked to say a little prayer to Allah

Qur'an 23:28 (All praise be to Allah who delivered us from an unjust people).

The water started pouring from the sky and gushing out of the land. (There is a spot marked in Masjid-e-Kufa where the water first started gushing out)

The ark started moving. Prophet Nuh's son who had refused to enter the ark thought he would be saved by climbing on a mountain and did not listen to his father. He was drowned.

Soon there was so much water that all that could be seen was the sky and water. There was a solar eclipse. It is related that the ark was pushed by the waves until it reached Mecca where it circled the Ka'ba. The whole world was submerged in water except the spot where Ka'ba stood.

Prophet Nuh (pbuh) was scared as the ark was tossed in the high waters. He recited "La Ilala Illallah' 1000* times. He also prayed as commanded by Allah "O my Lord! Make us land with a blessed landing for you are the best of all who cause to land".

When hearing the prayers from Prophet Nuh (pbuh) the earth swallowed in water, the sky stopped raining and the ark came to rest on Mount Juda **Qur'an 11:44.**

Prophet Nuh (pbuh) and the others came out at Mosul and here the foundation of the city of Madinatuth Thamaanin was laid. Prophet Nuh (pbuh) lived for quite a long time after this.

When the angel of death Izrail came to him Prophet Nuh (pbuh) asked him whether there was time for him to go into the shade from the sun. Izrail said there was and Prophet Nuh (pbuh) told him that the life of the world was just like passing from the sun into the shade i.e. like entering from one door and leaving through another.

Although he lived such a long time he never constructed a house for himself. He lived in a small hut.

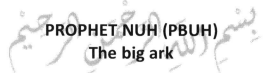

PROPHET NUH (PBUH)
The big ark

Prophet Nuh (pbuh) was sent by Allah to tell his people that there is only One God – Allah and to be good Muslims.

Prophet Nuh (pbuh) tried hard for many years but his people just laughed at him. They would put their fingers in their ears when he started to talk to them. Sometimes they would throw stones at him. The angel Jibrail used to come and help Prophet Nuh (pbuh) get up from under the pile of stones that were thrown athim.

Prophet Nuh (pbuh) complained to Allah that his people would just not listen. Allah told him to build a big ark (boat).

When the people saw Prophet Nuh (pbuh) and some of his family and friends building the ark, they laughed at him and teased him. There was no water near there and the sea and rivers were far away. Prophet Nuh (pbuh) carried on as Allah had ordered him to.

When the ark was ready, Allah told Prophet Nuh (pbuh) to take in it all the believers, and two of every kind of animals and birds.

As soon as they had entered the ark and the doors were shut, water began to pour from the skies and gush out of the land. All those who did not believe in Allah were drowned.

One of the sons of Prophet Nuh (pbuh) refused to come into the ark. He climbed into a high mountain thinking he would be saved but he toodrowned.

The ark was tossed around the big waves. Prophet Nuh (pbuh) prayed to Allah to make them land safely. He asked all the people in the ark to say:

(There is no God except Allah)

Allah answered his dua and made the earth swallow all the water. It stopped raining and the ark came to rest on a mountain called Judi.

PROPHET HUD (PBUH)

NAME: Hud (pbuh)
FATHER: Abdullah bin Riah bin Haloos bin
Aad bin Aus bin Saam bin Nuh.

Prophet Hud (pbuh) was sent to the people of Aad. Aad was situated in Ahqaaf (which is plural of Hoqf means a raised spot in the desert).   It is said to have been located in Yemen at the shores of the sea of Oman.

Prophet Hud (pbuh) was born amongst these people who were very strong and very rich. They however worshipped idols.

Prophet Hud (pbuh) spent a long time preaching to them to worship the One and Only God, their creator Allah.   The people were stubborn and refused to listen to him except very few.

Allah punished the people of Aad by sending a drought (no rain).   The people still would not believe and mocked Hud (pbuh) even beating him up. He warned them of a greater punishment but they just ignored him.

When the hardships became great they all came to Prophet Hud's house and asked him to pray for rain. He prayed for rain and the people had food again but they still refused to correct themselves.   In fact they defied Prophet Hud (pbuh) to bring the punishment that he had said Allah would send on them if he was true.

Prophet Hud (pbuh) told them that the knowledge of when was only with Allah.

Soon they saw a cloud coming towards them. Thinking it was rain they gathered underneath it.   However it was a blast of strong violent wind (like a cyclone) and it killed all the people of Aad.

Prophet Hud (pbuh) and a few believers were saved and it is said Hud (pbuh) moved to Hadhremaut (Yemen). It is said he died there and is buried there too.

PROPHET SALIH (PBUH)

NAME: Salih

FATHER: Abud bin Asif bin Nasikh bin Abud
 bin Hadir bin Thamood bin A'amir
 bin Saam binNuh

Prophet Salih (pbuh) was sent to the people of Thamood.   The tribe of Thamood were well to do people who lived in the valley of Hijr between Madina and Syria. They used to carve their homes of huge rocks in the mountains. The tribe of Thamood is also known as the second Aad. Allah had favoured them with wealth and bounties but they forgot him and worshipped idols.

Prophet Salih (pbuh) preached to the people for a long time urging them to abandon their idols and to worship Allah. They used to annually worship a piece of the mountain offering sacrifices it. They called Prophet Salih (pbuh) to bring a sign from Allah to them if he was one of the truthful ones.

Allah sent as a sign to them a she-camel and it was commanded by Allah that the she-camel would drink all the water of the spring one day and the people of Thamood would drink from it one day.

Never had the people seen such a camel who drink all the water of the spring on alternate days but still would not abandon their idols. Prophet Salih (pbuh) had also warned them that if they harmed the she camel they would be punished by Allah.

Their pride and stubbornness however caused them to kill the she-camel. They then came to Prophet Salih (pbuh) and said "O Salih, bring us what you threatened us with if you are of the messengers" **Qur'an 7:77**.

He asked them to repent (do tawbah) within three days but they only mocked him.

On the 4th day there was a thunder bolt from the sky and earthquake killing the

 people of Thamood. Prophet Salih (pbuh) and his few followersescaped.

Prophet Salih (pbuh) was greatly moved to see the dead bodies of his tribe and he returned and addresses the dead saying "O my people, indeed I did deliver to you the message of my Lord and did warn you but you did not heed the warners". **Qur'an 7:79**

PROPHET IBRAHIM (PBUH)

NAME: Ibrahim (pbuh)

FATHER: Tarookh bin Nahoor bin Sarooj bin
Reu bin Peleg bin Aber bin Salah bin
Arikshaz bin Saam bin Nuh

TITLE: Khalilullah (Friend of Allah)

CHILDREN: Ismail & Ishaaq (pbuh)

He was born in the time of the king called Namrud who claimed that he was God. An astrologer had told Namrud that there was soon to be a Prophet who would overthrow Namrud and invite people to Allah. Namrud afraid of losing his power ordered all men and women in the land to be separated so there would be no children born. He thought he could change the will of Allah. Prophet Ibrahim (pbuh) was born and his mother hid him in a cave outside the town where they lived until he was 13 yrs old. His mother felt it was safe to bring him into town then.

People used to worship idols (statues), stars, moon and the sun. Prophet Ibrahim (pbuh) told them to worship the creator of the sun, moon and stars. He also told them not to worship statues. One day when the people were out of town, he went to where the statues were kept and broke all of them leaving only the biggest one. When the people of the town came back they saw the broken statues and rushed towards Prophet Ibrahim (pbuh) saying "Have you done this to our Gods, Ibrahim?" **Qur'an 21:62**

Prophet Ibrahim (pbuh) wanted them to realise the helplessness of these statues and asked them to ask the biggest one. The people knew that their Gods could not answer and lowered their head in shame and said "You know full well that these (statues) speak not"
Qur'an 21:65

Prophet Ibrahim (pbuh) replied "Would you then worship that which can neither help nor harm you?" **Qur'an 21:66**

He wanted to show them the uselessness of their Gods but the people were stubborn. They did not want to admit defeat. They wanted to get rid of Prophet Ibrahim (pbuh).

A huge furnace was constructed and firewood was collected for a month. Prophet Ibrahim (pbuh) was placed in a catapult and flung into the fire. As he was being thrown into the fire several angels came to him offering to rescue him but Prophet Ibrahim (pbuh) said that was a matter between him and his Lord (Allah). In the Qur'an Allah says that he told the fire "O fire! Be cold and a safety to Ibrahim (pbuh)". **Qur'an 21:69**

Namrud was astounded when from the top of his palace he saw that the fire had turned into a garden.

After this Ibrahim (pbuh) left the city of Babul and migrated to Syria. From Syria he went to Ghazaza. On the way there a king presented Sarah (Prophet Ibrahim's wife) with a slave (maid) called Hajra. Sarah presented Hajra to Prophet Ibrahim (pbuh).Sarah did not have any children and Prophet Ibrahim (pbuh) prayed to Allah for achild.

"O my Lord! Grant me righteous (son)" **Qur'an 37:100**

Through Hajra Allah granted Prophet Ibrahim (pbuh) a son called Ismail. When Ismail was born Prophet Ibrahim (pbuh) was 86 yrs old. Sarah did not like this very much, so Prophet Ibrahim (pbuh) took Hajra and Ismail to the place now known as Makka and left them there.

There Hajra and her baby son Ismail soon ran out of water. Hajra ran in search of water between the two mountains of Safa and Marwa. Suddenly she saw a spring of water gush out under the heel of her son Ismail. The spring is still there today and is known as Zamzam (meaning lots of water).

Soon the tribe of Banu Jurham came and settled around there and the town of Makka grew. Prophet Ibrahim (pbuh) visited them often. When Ismail (pbuh) was 13 yrs old, Prophet Ibrahim (pbuh) dreamt that he was sacrificing Ismail (pbuh); it was a dream from Allah.

Prophet Ibrahim (pbuh) talked to Ismail about his dream and Ismail who too was to be a Prophet said that Prophet Ibrahim (pbuh) should do as Allah had commanded. On the way to Mina (where Ibrahim was to sacrifice Ismail) Shaytan tried to stop Ibrahim (pbuh) 3 times but it did not have any effect. Just as Prophet Ibrahim (pbuh) had thought that he had sacrificed Ismail (pbuh) (after passing a knife over his neck) he opened his blindfold and saw that Ismail was standing safe near him and in his place there was a Ram. Ibrahim (pbuh) thought that his sacrifice had not been accepted but he heard a voice which said:

"O Ibrahim, indeed you have proven true that dream, thus do we reward the doers of good".**Qur'an**

Prophet Ibrahim (pbuh) talked to Ismail about his dream and Ismail who too was to be a Prophet said that Prophet Ibrahim (pbuh) should do as Allah had commanded. On the way to Mina (where Ibrahim was to sacrifice Ismail) Shaytan tried to stop Ibrahim (pbuh) 3 times but it did not have any effect. Just as Prophet Ibrahim (pbuh) had thought that he had sacrificed Ismail (pbuh) (after passing a knife over his neck) he opened his blindfold and saw that Ismail was standing safe near him and in his place there was a Ram. Ibrahim (pbuh) thought that his sacrifice had not been accepted but he heard a voice which said:

"O Ibrahim, indeed you have proven true that dream, thus do we reward the doers of good".**Qur'an37:105**

We celebrate Eid-ul-Hajj (Adha) commemorating the above sacrifice of Ibrahim (pbuh) Allah says in the Qur'an "Never shall you achieve righteousness unless you spend (in the way of Allah) that which youlove most".**Qur'an 3:91**

Prophet Ibrahim (pbuh) and Ismail also made the Ka'ba as commanded by Allah near the grave of Hajra who had died. The place where Prophet Ibrahim (pbuh) stood is also there today and is known as Maqame Ibrahim. Allah softened the rock he was standing on to mould his footprint. Prophet Ibrahim (pbuh) prayed to Allah to make the Ka'ba safety for people, he also prayed for his progeny (children) to be good and to have leaders (Imams) from them.

Allah granted his prayers raising Prophet Muhammad (pbuh) from his progeny.

Even in the Torah (Old Testament) there is a verse about 12 Imams (leaders) from Ismail (pbuh) "And as for Ishmail, I have heard you; Behold I have blessed him and will make him fruitful and will multiply him exceedingly, 12 princes shall he beget and I shall make him a great nation".   **(Genesis 17:20)**

وَقُل رَّبِّ زِدْنِي عِلْمًا

PROPHET IBRAHIM (PBUH)
"O our Rabb! Accept this from us!"

They picked up the heavy stones one by one. The angel Jibrail showed them where to put each stone.

Soon the Ka'ba was nearly finished. Jibrail also showed them where to put the special black stone.

Prophet Ibrahim (pbuh) and his son Prophet Ismail (pbuh) worked very hard. Prophet Ibrahim (pbuh) used to stand on a stone. The stone moulded his footprints. Today it still stands near the Ka'ba and is known as Maqame Ibrahim.

When they finished building the Ka'ba, father and son raised their hands and prayed:

..."O our Lord! Accept this from us. Indeed You are the All-hearing and the All-Knowing."

Qur'an - Suratul Baqara 2:127

Prophet Ismail (pbuh) settled in Makka and lived there all his life. His mother Bibi Hajra (pbuh) is buried next to the Ka'ba.

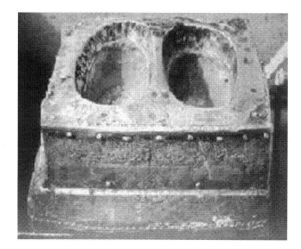

PROPHET IBRAHIM (PBUH)
The dream of Ibrahim

Prophet Ibrahim (pbuh) was resting not far from Makka on Mount Rahma in a place called Arafat when he had a dream.

He dreamt that he was sacrificing his son Prophet Ismail (pbuh).
For three days he had the same dream.

He loved Ismail (pbuh) very much but he realised that Allah wanted to test him. How much did he love Allah?

Ismail (pbuh) was thirteen years old. Prophet Ibrahim (pbuh) told Ismail (pbuh) about his dream. Ismail (pbuh) wanted his father to do what Allah wanted.

Prophet Ibrahim (pbuh) laid Ismail (pbuh) down. He tied his hands and feet and blindfolded him and himself.

He opened his eyes after he thought he had sacrificed his son but Lo and Behold! Standing near him safe and sound was Ismail (pbuh) and a ram (daddy sheep) was in the place of Ismail (pbuh)

Allah had accepted the sacrifice of Prophet Ibrahim (pbuh) and he had passed his test of faith.
We remember the sacrifice of Prophet Ibrahim (pbuh) on Eid ul Adha (Hajj).

PROPHET IBRAHIM (PBUH)
"O fire! Be cold and a safety to Ibrahim"

The people of the town where Prophet Ibrahim (pbuh) lived worshipped statues, the sun, the moon and the stars.

Prophet Ibrahim (pbuh) always told them to worship only Allah, the one and only God.
There is no God except Allah

The people did not listen to him. One day when all the people had gone out of the town to celebrate a festival, Prophet Ibrahim (pbuh) went to the place where they kept all the statues. He broke all of them except the biggest one and tied the axe which he used around the neck of the biggest statue.

When the people of the town came back they were very angry and asked Prophet Ibrahim (pbuh) who had broken the other statues. He told them to ask the biggest statue which was not broken. Of course the statue could not answer their question. The people realised that their gods (statues) were useless because they could not even protect themselves; but they were very stubborn and still did not want to believe that there is no god except Allah.

They decided to kill Prophet Ibrahim (pbuh).

A big bonfire was built and Prophet Ibrahim (pbuh) was thrown into the fire. Allah told the fire:
"….O fire! Be cold and safe for Ibrahim..."   **Qur'an – Suratul Ambiya 21:69**
The ruler who was called Namrud saw from the top of his palace that the fire had become a garden for Prophet Ibrahim (pbuh) but he still did not want to believe in Allah.
Prophet Ibrahim (pbuh) left and went away to another country.

Prophet Ibrahim (pbuh) loved having guests.

He would walk near the main road near his house every day and when he saw any traveller, he would invite them home for food and rest. On days, when there were no travellers, he would be unhappy.

Once, for three days no traveller passed by. Prophet Ibrahim (pbuh) was very sad. He too did not eat. Each morning he would go to the main road, hoping that someone would pass by.

After three days, he saw an old man on a camel. Prophet Ibrahim (pbuh) invited the man home. To his delight, the man accepted the invitation.
When they sat to eat, Prophet Ibrahim (pbuh) recited:

He noticed that the old man did not say anything. Prophet Ibrahim (pbuh) asked him why he did not remember Allah before eating. Was not Allah his Creator and the Provider of the food?

The old man replied that it was not a custom of his religion as he was one who worshipped fire. Prophet Ibrahim (pbuh) was annoyed and asked the man to leave his house.

As soon as he had sent the man away, the angel Jibrail came with a message from Allah. Jibrail told Prophet Ibrahim (pbuh) that Allah had been looking after that man despite him worshipping fire for seventy years. Could Prophet Ibrahim (pbuh) not tolerate him for one meal?
Feeling ashamed, Prophet Ibrahim (pbuh) ran after the old man. He apologised for his behaviour and returned home with him to complete their meal.

PROPHET IBRAHIM (PBUH)
Khalilullah

Prophet Ibrahim (pbuh) was given the title 'Khalilullah' which meant the friend of Allah.

When the angel of death came to Prophet Ibrahim (pbuh) and said that it was time for him to return to Allah; Prophet Ibrahim (pbuh) told him that he was a friend of Allah so why would a friend kill a friend.

Izrail, the angel of death took his message to Allah. The answer came:
"O Ibrahim! Does a friend refuse an invitation from a friend to come to Him?"

"Indeed we are from Allah and indeed to Him we will return." (2:156)

PROPHET ISMAIL (PBUH)
Zam Zam

Prophet Ibrahim (pbuh) was an old man when Allah granted him a son called Ismail (pbuh). He too was a prophet.

The mother of Prophet Ismail (pbuh) was Sayyida Hajra (pbuh). She was a very good lady.

Prophet Ibrahim (pbuh) took Sayyida Hajra (pbuh) and his son Prophet Ismail (pbuh) to a place which is today called Makka. He left them there as Allah had ordered him to do and went away.

Soon Sayyida Hajra (pbuh) found that all their food and water had finished. She went to look for water. There were two mountains called Safa and Marwa in Makka. She climbed up on the mountain of Safa first and looked around. She saw water and ran towards it until she reached the mountain of Marwa. Then she looked back and saw water again. She ran towards it until she reached Safa. She was seeing a mirage. But she did not give up! She ran back and forth seven times.

As she ran backwards and forwards, she used to glance towards her baby son Ismail to keep an eye on him. Suddenly she saw her baby son Ismail (pbuh) with a spring of water near his feet. The spring is still there today and it is called Zam Zam which means - Stop! Stop! (As this is what Sayyida Hajra said when she saw the water for she feared that her baby would drown). It may also mean 'lots of water'.

Because of the spring of Zam Zam many people came to live there and soon Makka became the central town of Arabia.

PROPHET LUT (PBUH) (LOT)

Prophet Lut (pbuh) was the cousin of Prophet Ibrahim (pbuh). Their mothers were sisters and Prophet Lut's (pbuh) own sister, Sarah, was Prophet Ibrahim's (pbuh) first wife. The two Prophets (pbuh) migrated together to Palestine, but later Prophet Lut (pbuh) settled in the district of Sodom in Jordan.

The people of Sodom were unsociable and treated strangers disgracefully. Anybody who passed through their area would be robbed of all his possessions. Their life was full of singing, merry-making and gambling. But by far the worst vice in their community was homosexuality, which was openly practised. The word sodomy is in fact a reference to the people of Sodom, who were the first to commit this despicable act. To guide these shameless people, Allah sent Prophet Lut (pbuh) to them. Prophet Lut (pbuh) did his utmost to teach the people about the evil of their ways. He preached to them the message of Allah and begged them to give up their lewd and disgusting customs.

However, after 30 years of guidance, only a handful of people had accepted his teaching while the rest remained engrossed in their sinful habits.

The Holy Qur'an says:

And (We sent) Lut, when he said to his people, "Why do you commit such indecent acts that have never been committed before by anyone in any of the worlds? Verily, you come to men in lust instead of women. Indeed you are a people who are guilty of excess." And they had no answer except that they said, "Turn him out of our town, he and his people seek to purify (themselves)."

Suratul A'raf, 7: 80 – 82

While Prophet Lut (pbuh) increased his efforts to try and guide the people, they wanted to expel him and his followers from the town. When he warned the people to fear the wrath of Allah for their indecent behaviour, they laughed and said that they did not care about it.

Finally Prophet Lut (pbuh) despaired of ever guiding the people. He was deeply ashamed when they forced travellers passing through the town to indulge in their vile acts, and prayed to Allah to deliver him and his family from the people of Sodom.

Finally, the punishment of Allah descended on these wretched people. Allah sent down a group of His angels, including Jibrail, to teach the people of Sodom a terrible lesson. The angels came down in human form and first visited Prophet Ibrahim (pbuh).

He thought they were travellers who were passing by his house, so he welcomed them and prepared a roasted calf for them. However, they did not touch their meals and their strange behaviour frightened Prophet Ibrahim (pbuh). At this point, the angels introduced themselves and said that they were on their way to punish the people of Lut. However, they also informed him of the good news that he would soon be blessed them with a son, (Prophet) Ishaaq (pbuh), and a grandson, (Prophet) Ya'qub (pbuh).

Prophet Ibrahim (pbuh) had not been able to have a child with his wife Sarah and the news delighted them.

Then, he remembered their other purpose.

"And when Ibrahim recovered from his awe and had received the good news, he began pleading with Us for Lut's people. Verily, Ibrahim was indeed forbearing, compassionate and often turned to Allah. (Allah said), "O Ibrahim, Forsake this (argument)! Indeed the decree of your Lord has already come to pass, and verily, they are about to receive a torment (which is) irreversible." **Suratu Hud, 11: 74 - 76**

The angels then changed themselves into handsome young men and left for Sodom. When they reached the town, they knocked at the door of Prophet Lut's (pbuh) house. Prophet Lut (pbuh) was very worried when he saw that he had guests who were handsome youths, because he knew very well what the habits of his people were. However, he could not turn them away and so he welcomed them to his house.

The Holy Qur'an says:

"And when Our Messengers came to Lut, he was grieved for them and felt himself powerless (to protect them) and they said, "Do not fear or grieve, we will deliver you and your people, except your wife. She shall be of those who stay behind. Verily, we are bringing upon the people of this town a punishment for their sins." And indeed We have left a clear sign of it for a people who understand". **Suratul 'Ankabut, 29: 33 - 35**

No sooner had the guests arrived than Prophet Lut's (pbuh) immoral wife signalled to the people that there were young men in her house.

The Holy Qur'an says:

And his people came rushing to him, those who had done evil deeds in the past. He (Lut) said, "O my people, here are my daughters (to marry) - they are purer for you, so guard against (the punishment of) Allah, and do not disgrace me about my guests. Is there not amongst you a single right minded man?" They said, "Indeed you know that we do not need your daughters and you very well know what we intend." **Suratul Hud 11: 78,79**

As the people surged towards the house, determined to satisfy their evil desires, Jibrail waved his arm at them and turned them blind. He then asked Prophet Lut (pbuh) to leave in the night with his family and the few virtuous people, but to leave his wife behind. As soon as they were safe, the angels brought the punishment of Allah on the town.

The Qur'an says:

"So the (violent) Blast seized them (while) entering upon dawn. Thus did We turn it (the town) upside down and rained down on them stones of baked clay. Verily, in this are signs for those who are heedful". **Suratul Hijr, 15: 73 – 75**

PROPHET YA'QUB (PBUH) (JACOB)

"And We bestowed on him (Ibrahim) Ishaaq, and Ya'qub as an additional gift, and made them righteous. And We made them leaders to guide (the people) by Our command; and We inspired them to perform good deeds and observe their moral obligations and pay Zakaa; and they obeyed Us".   **Suratul Ambiya, 21: 72,73**

Prophet Ishaaq (pbuh) was the younger son of Prophet Ibrahim (pbuh), by his wife Sarah. Prophet Ishaaq (pbuh) married his uncle's daughter Rafqa, and they had twin sons, Isu and Prophet Ya'qub (pbuh).

Prophet Ya'qub (pbuh) was much loved by his parents and this made his twin brother jealous. To prevent trouble between the brothers, Prophet Ishaaq (pbuh) advised Prophet Ya'qub (pbuh) to migrate from their home in Palestine to Fidan Aram, where his maternal uncle Labaan lived. In Fidan Aram he worked for his uncle and married his uncle's daughter.

Sometime later, he returned to Palestine, sent presents to his brother to indicate good-will, which were accepted and soon, the grudge between the brothers was forgotten.

Prophet Ya'qub (pbuh) decided to make his home in the land of Kanaan and Allah blessed him with twelve sons.

From his first wife Lay'ah, he had six sons - Yahuda, Roil, Sham'son, Lavi, Zialoon and Yashjaar. From his marriage to Lay'ah's younger sister Raheel he had one daughter, Diana, and two sons, Binyameen and Prophet Yusuf (pbuh). In addition, Prophet Ya'qub (pbuh) had two sons, Haad and Ashar from his marriage to Lay'ah's slave girl Zulfa, and a daughter, Danya and two sons, Don and Toftali from his marriage to Raheel's slave girl Maleha. His twelve sons became famously known as the "Grandchildren ofIshaaq"

Raheel died early and therefore Prophet Ya'qub (pbuh) always regarded her sons Binyameen and especially Prophet Yusuf (pbuh) with particular affection. His love for Prophet Yusuf (pbuh) was later to become a source of jealousy for his older sons.

PROPHET YUSUF (PBUH) (JOSEPH)

Prophet Yusuf (pbuh) was the son of Prophet Ya'qub (pbuh). Prophet Yusuf (pbuh) had 11 brothers.

Prophet Yusuf (pbuh) once dreamt that eleven stars and the sun and moon were prostrating to him. He related the dream to his father. Prophet Ya'qub (pbuh) realised that the dream outlined his son's destiny and greatness and cautioned him not to tell his brothers about the dream.

Prophet Yusuf's (pbuh) brothers were jealous of the favour that he enjoyed in their father's eyes and resolved to somehow get rid of him. Whenever they took their goats out for grazing they would ask their father if Prophet Yusuf (pbuh) could accompany them. Prophet Ya'qub (pbuh) always refused, saying that the boy was too young. When Prophet Yusuf (pbuh) reached the age of 16, his brothers insisted that he was now old enough to accompany them. With reluctance, their father agreed to let them take Prophet Yusuf (pbuh) with them.

As soon as they were far enough from home, they began to plot about how to dispose of Prophet Yusuf (pbuh). Then, they came across a dry well. They removed Prophet Yusuf's (pbuh) shirt, and threw him into the well. Ignoring their young brother's pleas, they heartlessly left him to die of hunger. On the way back, they slaughtered a goat and stained Prophet Yusuf's (pbuh) shirt with its blood. They arrived home weeping and told their father that while they were grazing their sheep, a wolf came and ate Prophet Yusuf (pbuh). He did not believe their story and could do nothing but remainedpatient.

Meanwhile a caravan of traders passing by the well stopped to draw some water. They were surprised to see Prophet Yusuf (pbuh) come up holding the bucket. They hid him with their merchandise and sold him to some slave traders for a few pieces of silver.

Thus Prophet Yusuf (pbuh) arrived in Egypt. At the slave market the buyers were all attracted by Prophet Yusuf (pbuh), who was a very handsome young man. News of this remarkable youth swept through the city. The Aziz (Governor of Egypt and Chief Officer of the King), whose name was Fotifar, offered a price that none could match. He brought Prophet Yusuf (pbuh) home and told his wife Zulaykha that they would adopt him as their son.

Zulaykha, however, was taken by Prophet Yusuf (pbuh) and called him to her room. When Prophet Yusuf (pbuh) backed away from her she ripped his shirt from behind. At the door they met the Aziz. On seeing her husband, Zulaykha tried to blame Yusuf (pbuh) by claiming that he had tried to lay a hand on her. Before the Aziz could get angry on Prophet Yusuf (pbuh), a baby spoke up from the cradle, saying:

"...and a witness from her own household testified, "If his shirt is torn from the front, then she speaks the truth and he is of the liars. And if his shirt is torn from behind, then she lies and he is of thetruthful ones". **Suratu Yusuf, 12: 26,27**

The shirt was, of course, torn from behind, and the Aziz was extremely angry with his wife. The women of the city heard about Zulaykha's actions and began to gossip and make fun of her. To explain her attraction she decided to let them see Prophet Yusuf (pbuh) themselves. She called forty of them to the palace for a meal. As soon as they all had a knife to cut some fruit, she called Prophet Yusuf (pbuh) into the room on some excuse. So dazzled were they by his beauty and presence, that they cut their fingers in their distraction and exclaimed, "This is not a human being - he must be anangel!"

Due to continued pressure from his wife Zulaykha, the Aziz of Egypt decided to imprison Prophet Yusuf (pbuh), despite his innocence. The reason he gave was that people would forget the actions of his wife while Prophet Yusuf (pbuh) lay in prison, and her dignity would be restored.

On the same day that Prophet Yusuf (pbuh) was put into prison, two other men were also imprisoned. One used to serve the king wine, while the other was the royal cook. Both men had been accused of trying to poison the king. On the following day, the wine-server said to Prophet Yusuf (pbuh), "I saw in a dream that I was crushing grapes to make wine for the king". The cook said, "I dreamt that I was carrying some bread in a basket on my head and birds were pecking at the bread".

Both men saw that Prophet Yusuf (pbuh) was a pious person and asked him if he could interpret their dreams. Prophet Yusuf (pbuh) took this opportunity to teach about Allah. Of their dreams he said, "O my prison-mates! The man who dreamt that he was crushing grapes will soon be released from here and will go back to his previous post. The second one, who carried the bread on his head in the dream, will be executed and the birds will start to eat his brain."

Prophet Yusuf (pbuh) thought of getting himself released from prison through the wine- server, and told him to remind the king of his innocence when he saw him. The dreams of both men came true just as Prophet Yusuf (pbuh) had foretold. One of the captives was released while the other was hanged. Unfortunately, the wine-server forgot all that Prophet Yusuf (pbuh) had told him to convey to the king.

The king had a dream which is related in the Qur'an:
'The king dreamt that seven lean cows were eating seven fat ones and that there were seven green ears of corn and seven dry ones. He asked the nobles to tell him the meaning of his dream if they were able to. They replied, "It is a confused dream and we do not know the meaning of such dreams." **Suratu Yusuf, 12: 43,44**

The king was very concerned about the meaning of his dream and even though his wise men thought over it seriously, they could not make sense of it. The king's dream became a means of the liberation of Prophet Yusuf (pbuh) from prison

As soon as the wine-server heard about the dream he was reminded of his time in prison and remembered the powers of his cell-mate. He also remembered that Prophet Yusuf (pbuh) had asked him to tell the king of his innocence. He approached the king and got his permission to see Prophet Yusuf (pbuh).

Prophet Yusuf (pbuh) interpreted the dream saying, "For seven years the crops will yield abundant grain for the people of Egypt. After that there will be a famine for seven years during which all the grain lying in the storehouses will be finished and people will starve. Therefore, the people should try to grow as much extra grain as possible so that it would stand them in good stead during the time of famine".

On hearing this very reasonable and sensible interpretation of his dream from the wine- server, the king was delighted. He ordered that Prophet Yusuf (pbuh) be brought before him so he could make good use of his wisdom in solving his problems.

Although he had been in prison for so long, Prophet Yusuf (pbuh) refused to leave until he had proved his innocence. He said to the courtiers, "I will not come out of the prison until the king makes enquiries about my case. Tell the king to ask the wives of the noble men about the time when they cut their fingers on seeing me".

They all confessed the truth and Zulaykha, the wife of the Aziz, also testified that Prophet Yusuf (pbuh) was innocent. Thus, Prophet Yusuf (pbuh) was released from prison with his honour restored.

Allah in the Qur'an says:
'The king ordered his men to bring Yusuf before him; he wanted to grant him a high office. The king said to him, "From now on you will be an honoured and trusted person amongst us." Yusuf said, "Put me in charge of the treasuries of the land, I know how to manage them." **Suratu Yusuf, 12: 54,55**

Prophet Yusuf (pbuh) thus became the Aziz of Egypt and began his new duties without delay. He was determined that when the famine arrived, nobody should starve. During the first seven years, Prophet Yusuf (pbuh) allocated extra money to the farmers in the most fertile areas of the Nile, so that they would be able to grow the maximum amount of grain. He also ordered the construction of huge storehouses (granaries), capable of storing several hundred tons of the surplus grain. By the time the seven years were over, the granaries were full.

After that the country was hit by a severe drought. However, due to the foresight and planning of Prophet Yusuf (pbuh), the country did not face a shortage of food. The famine also extended to the lands of Palestine and Kanaan where Prophet Ya'qub (pbuh) lived with his sons. One day he called them and said, "My sons! We are in great distress due to the famine. You may go to the Aziz of Egypt whose reputation as a kind and just person has spread everywhere in the country. Leave Binyameen with me for company so that I may not be lonely." As commanded by their father, the brothers of Prophet Yusuf (pbuh) set off for Egypt to purchase grain and bring it back toKanaan.

When his brothers arrived in Egypt, Prophet Yusuf (pbuh) was very pleased to see them. They did not recognize him at all, never expecting that he was alive.
Prophet Yusuf (pbuh) was disappointed not to see Binyameen. He provided them with enough wheat for their needs and had their money put back in their bags secretly. He also asked them to bring their other brother the nexttime.
The Qur'an says: "Yusuf's brothers came to him and when they entered his court, he recognized them. They did not know him. And when he gave them the provisions, he said, "Next time, bring me your other brother from your father. As you can see, I give each of you a certain amount of grain, I am a polite host. If you do not bring him, do not come to us for we shall not give you any more grain". **Suratu Yusuf, 12: 58 - 60**

On their return home, the brothers told their father of Prophet Yusuf's hospitality. When they were in need of grain again they returned to Egypt, this time with Binyameen. Prophet Yusuf (pbuh) was extremely happy to see his younger brother and revealed his identity to Binyameen. However, he asked Binyameen not to tell their brothers anything of their conversation.

Prophet Yusuf (pbuh) made a plan mentioned in Suratu Yusuf, which enabled Binyameen to stay behind. He ordered his men to put a gold cup belonging to the king in Binyameen's baggage. The brothers of Prophet Yusuf (pbuh) had not gone very far when they were stopped and accused of stealing. They denied this, and said that if anyone of them was found guilty of theft, he could be held as a slave by Prophet Yusuf (pbuh). The caravan was searched, and the cup was found in the bag of Binyameen.

When the brothers were brought before Prophet Yusuf (pbuh), he said, "According to your own words, we will now detain Binyameen with us."

They replied, "O Aziz of Egypt! Our father is old and weak. You may detain any of us, but not Binyameen." However, Prophet Yusuf (pbuh) said that he could not detain anyone who was not guilty. The brothers had no choice but to leave for Kanaan. The eldest brother, Yahuda, refused to return without Binyameen. He remained behind in Egypt, rather than face his father.

When the brothers returned to Kanaan and told Prophet Ya'qub (pbuh) what had happened, he was heartbroken. He asked his sons to immediately return to Egypt to look for both Prophet Yusuf (pbuh) and Binyameen.

Prophet Yusuf (pbuh) reminded them of how badly they had treated their brother Yusuf. On hearing this, the brothers hung their heads in shame and asked Prophet Yusuf (pbuh) for his forgiveness. He said, "You need not be frightened of me. Allah may forgive you your sins.

Now take my shirt and cover my father's face with it, so that he may regain his lost sight. Then return to me with all your family."

After getting his eyesight back and hearing the good news of his son, Prophet Ya'qub (pbuh) decided to go to Egypt immediately. As a token of their thanks to Allah, his parents and brothers did sajda.

Thus Allah made true the dream of Prophet Yusuf (pbuh), when he had seen eleven stars and the sun and the moon in prostration in front of him. At the request of his son, Prophet Ya'qub (pbuh) settled in Egypt with his family, and their clan came to be known as the Bani Isra'il. Prophet Ya'qub (pbuh) lived in Egypt for 17 years and died at the age of 147. Prophet Yusuf (pbuh) breathed his last some years later at the age of 110 years, and his kingdom passed into the hands of the Fir'aun.

PROPHET AYYUB (PBUH) (JOB)

Prophet Ayyub (pbuh) was the grandson of Prophet Ishaaq (pbuh) son of Prophet Ibrahim (pbuh) and his wife was the granddaughter of Prophet Yusuf (pbuh). He was a wealthy and generous man with large flocks of sheep and a lot of land. He had many children and was well respected by his people.

He was devoted to Allah.

On seeing the devotion of Prophet Ayyub (pbuh) to Allah, Shaytan decided to try to lead him astray. Since he was dealing with a Prophet, Shaytan requested Allah for power over Prophet Ayyub's (pbuh) affairs and said,

"O Allah, while Ayyub enjoys your blessings he remains grateful to you. But give me control over his affairs and I will make him turn away from you."

Allah was fully aware of the patience and steadfastness of Prophet Ayyub (pbuh), but as a trial for His Prophet and as a lesson for mankind, he granted Shaytan's request.

Shaytan caused the destruction of all Prophet Ayyub's (pbuh) animals and property and worse of all, he killed his children as well. However, Prophet Ayyub (pbuh) turned to Allah with even greater intensity than before.

When Shaytan saw his plot defeated, he caused Prophet Ayyub (pbuh) to lose his health and be got with a severe disease. Seeing the troubles befalling Prophet Ayyub (pbuh), his people began saying that he must had done something awful to incur the punishment of Allah and they began to avoid him. Finally he was exiled from his community and had to leave the town. Prophet Ayyub (pbuh) began to live in the wilderness and passed his time praying to Allah. His only companion was his wife Rahma, who supported them by doing odd-jobs in people's houses.

Several years passed and Shaytan watched helplessly as Prophet Ayyub (pbuh) remained steadfast in his devotion and prayers to Allah. Finally, he decided that he would try Prophet Ayyub's (pbuh) patience through his wife. One day Shaytan came in the form of a human being to Rahma and told her that he knew of a way to cure her husband of his terrible disease. He told her to take a sheep and slaughter it in his name instead of the Name of Allah. He claimed that its meat would immediately cure Prophet Ayyub (pbuh). When she came back and suggested this treatment to her husband, he instantly realised what had happened. He reminded her that they were being tried and was cross with her, vowing to punish her for her evil suggestion.

Finally, Prophet Ayyub (pbuh) turned to Allah and complained about Shaytan's repeated efforts to make him forsake his beliefs.

"(Remember) Ayyub when he called to his Lord, "I am afflicted with distress and You are the Most Compassionate of all." So We heard his cry and relieved him of the misery he was in".

Suratul Ambiya, 21: 83, 84

Allah accepted the prayers of Prophet Ayyub (pbuh) and cured him of all his troubles. "Stamp your foot on the ground. This stream is for you to wash with, (and) a cool and (refreshing) drink." And we gave him his family and more like them; a mercy from Us and a reminder for those with understanding. And it was said to him, "Take in your hand a bunch of (thin) sticks (like fibre) and strike (your wife) with it, so as not to break your oath." Verily, We found him steadfast, an excellent servant. Verily, he turned to Us often".

Suratus Saad, 38: 42 - 44

Prophet Ayyub (pbuh) struck the ground with his foot and a stream of water came out. When he washed himself with the water he saw that his sickness disappeared and he returned to normal. His wife Rahma was worried about him, but when she returned she was amazed to see him restored to his former health.

Prophet Ayyub (pbuh) was happy at seeing his wife but after a time, he remembered his vow to punish her. But Allah revealed to him that he should strike her with a soft lash so as to literally fulfil his vow, but not to hurt her at all because she had faithfully served him in his time of trial. Allah then restored Prophet Ayyub (pbuh) to his former prosperity. He was blessed with many more children.

PROPHET SHU'AYB (PBUH)

Prophet Ibrahim (pbuh) had a son called Midian who married one of the daughters of Prophet Lut (pbuh). Allah granted them lots of children and they settled in a place which was later to be called Midian (Madyan). It was situated on the outskirts of Hijaz but within the borders of Syria.

Prophet Shu'ayb (pbuh) was sent by Allah to the people of Madyan. They were business people who were not fair in their dealings. They used to use wrong measures of weight i.e. give less for what they had charged (cheat their customers), and also used to steal. This was how they made a profit in their businesses.

When Prophet Shu'ayb (pbuh) told them to serve none but Allah and to stop cheating and stealing from people, they made fun of him because they did not want to lose their profits.

Prophet Shu'ayb (pbuh) is known as 'Khatîbul Ambiya' because his sermons (lectures) were very beautifully said, making people want to hear. The people of Madyan however, turned a deaf ear saying he was a liar. He also had a staff which would lower the height of any mountain so that he could climb on it with ease. It is said that it was the same staff that he gave to Prophet Musa (pbuh) with which Prophet Musa (pbuh) parted the Red Sea with Allah's permission. The people of Madyan let loose dogs on Prophet Shu'ayb (pbuh) and his followers and threatened to kill them.

Prophet Shu'ayb (pbuh) was very disappointed. He prayed to Allah to punish them. Allah accepted his dua and an earthquake shook Madyan. The whole city was flattened to the ground and only Prophet Shu'ayb (pbuh) and his followers were saved.

After that Prophet Shu'ayb (pbuh) was sent to the town of Ayka which was near Madyan. There the people said he was under a magic spell and not one followed his teachings.

Eventually Allah punished them too by sending intense heat to the town. For seven days the heat scorched them after which they saw a cloud coming towards them. All the people rushed to take shelter under it only to be rained with fire from the heavens and the people of Ayka were no more.

PROPHET MUSA (PBUH) (MOSES)

The family of Prophet Ya'qub (pbuh) who had settled in Egypt grew to a large number and were called the Bani Isra'il

After several centuries, a man called Firawn came to power in Egypt. He was alarmed to see that the Bani Isra'il had become so many. He started making life difficult for them. His oppression on them increased when an astrologer told him that a boy would be born from the Bani Isra'il who would destroy Firawn's kingdom. On hearing this, Firawn ordered that every male child born to the Bani Isra'il should bekilled.

When Prophet Musa (pbuh) was born, his mother hid him to protect him from the king's soldiers. Allah inspired her to put her baby in a water proof box and cast him into the waters of the Nile. She did this, and then sent her daughter to follow the little 'box' and see where it went. Firawn's wife – Aasiya found the box and asked Firawn if they could adopt the child as their own. Despite his misgivings, he agreed to her request and called some women to feed the crying child. However, the baby refused milk from all the women who came to feed him. In the meantime the sister came forward and offered to introduce a woman who she was certain the child would accept. Firawn asked for the woman to be brought and thus Prophet Musa (pbuh) was reunited with his mum.

Once as a youth Prophet Musa (pbuh) saw two men fighting. One was from Bani Isra'il, and shouted for help. Prophet Musa (pbuh) came to his rescue and struck the other man unintentionally killing him. He was seen by one of Firawn's men who had reported him.
Prophet Musa (pbuh) knew he had to leave the town.

He walked for a long time without any destination and finally reached Madain. He rested near a well and saw two women waiting their turn to get water whilst some shepherds got theirs. Prophet Musa (pbuh) helped them get some water. One of the women returned and told him that her father wished to thank him for his help. He went with her to her house and discovered that her father was Prophet Shu'ayb (pbuh).

Prophet Musa (pbuh) stayed with Prophet Shu'ayb and worked for him for 10 years eventually marrying his daughter Safura. He then left for Egypt with his wife. It was a cold winter's night – suddenly he saw a fire in the distance.

He asked his wife to remain where she was and headed for the fire, thinking to bring some of it back to give them relief from the bitter cold. When he reached

Mount Sinai he saw that the flames were coming from a green tree. Suddenly, a voice said:

"O Musa, I am your Lord! Take off your shoes for you have stepped on to the sacred valley of Tuwa." As Prophet Musa (pbuh) obeyed, he heard the voice ask him to throw his staff into the ground. At once it changed into a snake, scaring him. He was then commanded to lift the snake without fear and as he did so, it changed back into astick.

Next he was commanded to put his hand under his armpit. When he drew it out again, his hand glowed with a dazzling light, brilliant like the sun. The voice said to him, "O Musa!

These are the two great Signs of your Lord. Go back to Firawn and his people and invite them towards your Lord!" Prophet Musa (pbuh) requested that his brother, Prophet Harun (pbuh) accompany him and Allah agreed to his request.

Prophet Musa (pbuh) told Firawn that he was a Messenger of Allah. Firawn rejected this claim and then reminded Prophet Musa (pbuh) that he had brought him up and he accused him of having run away after committing a murder. Prophet Musa (pbuh) argued that he had only been raised away from his own family because his mother had been forced to abandon him in fear of his life. He also said that he had not intentionally killed anyone.

The miracles of Prophet Musa (pbuh) frightened Firawn and he asked his ministers for advice. They assured him that Prophet Musa and Harun (pbuh) were magicians. All the magicians of the land were called and when they threw their ropes on the ground, they began moving like snakes. Prophet Musa (pbuh) cast his staff down and his serpent ate all the pieces of rope. The magicians immediately realised that they were witnessing a miracle. Immediately, they went into sajda saying, "We believe in the Rabb of Musa".
Firawn threatened to kill them but they would not budge.

Firawn increased his oppression of the Bani Isra'il. Prophet Musa (pbuh) warned him of the punishment from Allah but he did not listen. Soon the country was hit by famine. Swarms of locusts ate away the crops. The river Nile flooded its banks and people were afflicted with lice and tumours. The people rushed to Prophet Musa (pbuh) asking him to pray for their relief and promised to believe in Allah but when they were cured, they returned to their idol worship.

Finally, Allah commanded Prophet Musa (pbuh) to take his people away:

"We commanded Musa, "Journey by night with Our creatures, and strike a dry path for them through the sea. Do not fear being overtaken by Firawn nor have dread of anything. Firawn followed them with his army, but the sea overpowered and engulfed them. Firawn had led his people astray and did not rightly guide them." **Suratu TaHa, 20: 77 - 79**

In the final moments of his life Firawn recognised the Greatness of Allah and he cried out that there is no god but the Rabb of Musa, and that he was a believer. Firawn and his people drowned, their bodies were thrown on the shore as a sign to humankind. The preserved body of Firawn can be seen in the Cairo museum even today as a lasting lesson.

Prophet Musa (pbuh) had promised the Bani Isra'il a book of guidance from Allah. On their way to Palestine, Allah commanded Prophet Musa (pbuh) that once they left Egypt he would bring to them a Divine Book for their guidance. He commanded Prophet Musa (pbuh) to come to Mount Sinai. The Qur'an says:

"We made an appointment of thirty nights with Musa to which we added ten more, so the term set by the Lord was completed in forty nights. Musa said to Harun, his brother, "Deputise for me among my people. Act rightly and do not follow the path of the mischief- makers". **Suratul A'raaf, 7:142**

When Prophet Musa (pbuh) returned with the Tawrat he saw that a man called Samiri had made a golden calf by collecting gold from the people of Bani Isra'il, and then sprinkled into its mouth some dust that he had collected from under the feet of the angel Jibrail, whom he had seen on the day that Firawn was drowned. The addition of the dust made the golden calf seem to make noises. The sight of his people worshipping a golden calf made Prophet Musa (pbuh) furious. The people said they had been misguided by Samiri and did tawba. The calf was melted and thrown into the sea.

After a long journey, the Bani Isra'il finally came near Palestine.

The Qur'an says: "When Musa told his people, "Recall Allah's favours to you. He made Messengers and kings out of your own people and gave you what He had not given others. Enter the Sacred Promised Land. Do not return to disbelief lest you become losers".

They said, "Musa, a strong race of people is living there. We shall never go there unless they leave the land first." **Suratul Ma'ida 5: 20 - 22**

Despite Prophet Musa's (pbuh) attempts to persuade them, they refused to move into Palestine. Instead, they said to him, "You and your Lord should go there and not we. We will stay away while you fight with the rulers and the people of Palestine. After the land is cleared of people, we will walk onto it".

As a result of their disobedience, the Bani Isra'il wandered in the wilderness for forty years. During these forty years a new generation of stronger people replaced the older demoralised one. Prophet Musa (pbuh) and Prophet Harun (pbuh) had died but Yusha' bin Nun, a successor of Prophet Musa (pbuh), led the Bani Isra'il and finally conquered Palestine.

PROPHET MUSA (PBUH)
The baby in the wooden box

Firawn was furious!! His astrologer (a person who forecasts what will happen in the future) had just told him that a baby was to be born who would be the king of Egypt and will take the place of Firawn.

Firawn ordered his soldiers to kill all the baby boys born in the land.

The mother of Prophet Musa (pbuh) was very worried. She was going to have her baby soon. She prayed to Allah to keep her baby safe.

When Prophet Musa (pbuh) was born, his mother went to the carpenter and asked him to make a waterproof box. He made her a box out of wood and lined it so the water would not seep in. She placed Prophet Musa (pbuh) in the box and let the box float down the river. She knew that Allah would keep him safe as He had given her the idea.

Firawn's wife, Sayyida Aasiya, found the box and when she opened it she saw the most beautiful baby she had ever seen. She had no children of her own and she asked Firawn if she could keep the baby as her own. Firawn agreed.

The baby however would not take milk from anyone. Prophet Musa's sister was watching all this. She went to Sayyida Aasiya and said that she knew someone who was very good with children. Aasiya agreed for her to bring the lady. Prophet Musa's (pbuh) sister ran back to her mother and took her to Sayyida Aasiya. As soon as prophet Musa (pbuh) saw his mother he took milk from her. Sayyida Aasiya asked her to look after the baby.

Allah had saved Prophet Musa (pbuh). He was brought up in the palace of Firawn, looked after by his own mother.

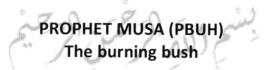

PROPHET MUSA (PBUH)
The burning bush

It was a cold night in the desert! Prophet Musa (pbuh) and his family were tired and very cold. Suddenly Prophet Musa (pbuh) saw a light. He told his wife to stay where she was and he would go and see what it was. If it was fire he would bring some back and they would be able to keep themselves warm. As he came near the light he saw that it was indeed a fire but the fire was burning from a green bush.

Suddenly a voice told him:
"O Musa! I am your Lord!...
I have chosen you to be My messenger..."

Allah then asked him:
"And what is this in your hand O Musa? Prophet Musa (pbuh) replied:
"This is my staff, I rest on it and I beat down leaves for my sheep, and use it for other things..."
Allah said:
"Throw it down O Musa!"

When Prophet Musa (pbuh) threw it down it became a running snake. Allah asked him to pick it up but Prophet Musa (pbuh) was a little scared. Allah told him not to be frightened and when Prophet Musa (pbuh) picked it up it became a staff again.

Allah then asked him to place his hand under his armpit. When Prophet Musa (pbuh) did that and took it out again there was a bright shining light onit.

These were the great miracles given to Prophet Musa (pbuh) by Allah.

Allah then asked him to go to Firawn to tell him there was only one God - Allah because Firawn used to claim that he himself was a God.

Prophet Musa (pbuh) asked Allah if he could take his brother Prophet Harun (pbuh) with him as his helper. Allah allowed him to do so.

PROPHET MUSA (PBUH)
Let my people go!

Prophet Musa (pbuh) and Prophet Harun (pbuh) went to see Firawn as Allah had commanded.

When they met Firawn they told him to believe in Allah. "And who is the Lord of you two? O Musa!" Firawn asked.

Prophet Musa (pbuh) told Firawn about Allah but Firawn just made fun of them.

Prophet Musa (pbuh) showed Firawn the miracles that Allah had given him. His staff which turned into a snake and his hand which when put under his armpit had a shining white light. Firawn still would not believe.

Firawn was very cruel to the people of Bani Isra'il. He was using them as slaves. Prophet Musa (pbuh) told him to let his people, the Bani Isra'il go but Firawn refused and made them work even harder.

Allah sent his punishment on the people of Firawn. He sent a storm of locusts and frogs everywhere, worms that got into people's noses and clothes. The river Nile turned to blood. Every time a punishment came Firawn would agree to let the Bani Isra'il go but when it was over he would say: "NO!"

Finally Allah told Prophet Musa (pbuh) to take the people away at night. At last they were on their way. When they got to the river Nile, Prophet Musa (pbuh), hit the river with his staff and 12 roads appeared for them to crosson.

Firawn and his soldiers were chasing them but when they got onto the roads in the river the waves folded over them and they were drowned.

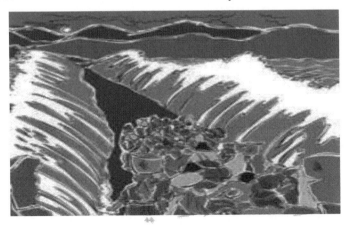

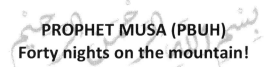

PROPHET MUSA (PBUH)
Forty nights on the mountain!

Prophet Musa (pbuh) climbed Mount Sinai to keep his appointment with Allah to be on the mountain for 40 nights.

He had left his brother Prophet Harun (pbuh) in charge to look after the Bani Isra'il.

Allah gave Prophet Musa (pbuh) some rules for the people to follow so they could be good Muslims. The rules were written in a book called the TAWRAT.

Some of the rules were:
Don't worship any gods except Allah Do not steal.
Do not lie.
Do not blame anyone wrongly.

Whilst Prophet Musa (pbuh) was on the mountain, the Bani Isra'il did not listen to Prophet Harun (pbuh). They listened to a bad man called Samiri who told them to make a statue of a cow out of gold and to worship it.

When Prophet Musa (pbuh) came back he was very angry. He burnt the statue and threw the ashes into the sea.

He asked the people to ask for forgiveness from Allah.

PROPHET KHIDR (PBUH)

Prophet Khidr (pbuh) was sent to preach about the oneness of Allah, His messengers and divine books. One of his signs was that whatever he touched, dry wood or hard earth, it would turn green, hence the name Khidr.

The humility of Prophet Khidr (pbuh) is such that he is reported to have said: "Whenever I said to myself that I now know all Allah's friends, the same day I saw a friend of Allah whom I did not know."

Imam Ali Zaynul Abideen (pbuh) has said the Prophet Khidr's (pbuh) last advice to Prophet Musa (pbuh) was;

Never blame anyone for your sins for the most favourable acts before Allah are:
- Moderation in giving away
- Forgiveness in power
- Leniency towards the 'abd of Allah, for whoever is lenient towards people, Allah too will be lenient towards him on the Day of Judgement.
- Fear of Allah is the secret of all wisdom.

Prophet Khidr (pbuh) is still alive and is reported to be present at Hajj every year.

PROPHET ILYAS (PBUH)

Prophet Ilyas (pbuh) was a messenger sent to Ba'albak in East Damascus. The people there did not believe him and intended to kill him but he escaped from them taking refuge in a cave.

Just like Prophet Khidr (pbuh), Prophet Ilyas (pbuh) is still alive. He is believed to travel in the deserts guiding those who get lost.

Prophet Khidr (pbuh) and Prophet Ilyas (pbuh) are said to meet in Masjide Quba on Eid ul Adha every year. They are also said to meet in Baytul Muqaddas during the month of Ramadhan every year, perform Hajj and meet in Arafat.

PROPHET YUNUS (PBUH)
The Big Fish

The people of Ninevah just would not listen. Allah had sent Prophet Yunus (pbuh) to them to tell them to believe in Him and to be good Muslims. Prophet Yunus (pbuh) tried very hard but the people would laugh at him and just not listen.

Prophet Yunus (pbuh) got so fed up that he decided to leave the town of Ninevah. He went to the seashore and when he saw a boat leaving he boarded it and sailed away. Soon the sea became rough and the waves rose high as a storm hit them. The wind was blowing hard and the boat was being tossed from side to side.

The people on the boat decided to throw one man out to make the boat lighter. They drew lots and the name of Prophet Yunus (pbuh) came. He was thrown into the sea. Allah sent a big fish which swallowed Prophet Yunus (pbuh) He found himself in the darkness of the tummy of the big fish. Prophet Yunus (pbuh) realised his mistake of leaving the people of Ninevah.

He prayed to Allah asking for forgiveness. He said;

.... There is no god except You; Glory be to You; Indeed I have done wrong. Suratul Ambiya 21:87

Allah accepted his dua and told the big fish to drop Prophet Yunus (pbuh) on the seashore.

Prophet Yunus (pbuh) was feeling very sick. Allah made special plants to grow around him and give him shade until he was better. When he was better he went back to the people of Ninevah and started telling them about Allah. Finally, they believed in Allah.

LUQMAN (PBUH)

Luqman was an extremely pious man and used to mostly remain silent while he pondered about the nature of life. Once his master passed by him and said: "O Luqman! Why do you sit alone so much? You would better associate withpeople.

Luqman said: "Sitting alone is better for meditation which is the path to Janna."

During the last few years of his life, he withdrew from people and is believed to have passed away at the time of Prophet Yunus. He is buried in Palestine.

The Holy Prophet (pbuh) is reported to have said that although Luqman was not a prophet, he was a servant of Allah who meditated a great deal, enjoyed certainty, loved Allah and Allah too love him and favoured him by giving him wisdom.

His words of wisdom have been mentioned in the Qur'an in **Suratu Luqman 31: 12 – 18** "Indeed We gave to Luqman wisdom, saying, "Be grateful to Allah; for whoever is grateful, indeed he is only grateful for his own self; and whoever is ungrateful, (it is to the discredit of his own self); Indeed Allah is Self Sufficient, the Most Praised."

"And when Luqman said to his son while he counselled him: "O my son! Do not associate anything with Allah, for verily associating (anything) with Allah is the greatest sin"."

"O my son! verily if it is even the very weight of the grain of a mustard seed (closed) in (even) a rock, or (be it high) in the heavens or (buried deep) in the earth, Allah will bring it to light; Allah is All Subtle (Lateef), AllAware."

"O my son! Establish salaa and enjoin the good and forbid the evil, and be patient against what befalls you; indeed this is the task of steadfastness. And do not turn your face to people (in scorn) and do not walk proudly in the earth; verily Allah does not like any self-conceited boaster.

And be moderate (modest) and lower your voice; indeed the most unpleasant of voices is the braying of the donkeys."

PROPHET DAWUD (PBUH)

Prophet Musa (pbuh) had saved the Bani Isra'il from Firawn and brought them to Palestine where they still had to fight with the Philistines who chased them out of their homes. In the last battle, the sacred box which had the original tablets of the Tawrat was lost. The Bani Isra'il felt quite lost.

They spent many years with no land or homes. Finally they approached Prophet Samuel (pbuh) and asked him to appoint a strong king for them so that they could get back their land. On the command of Allah, Prophet Samuel (pbuh) appointed Taalut (Saul) as their king. The Bani Isra'il did not like the choice, saying that Taalut was a poor and unknown man.

However, Prophet Samuel (pbuh) informed them that Taalut had been chosen because
of his knowledge, wisdom and strength, and he would lead them to victory.

It took Taalut 20 years to find the sacred box which had the Tawrat and once it was given back to the Bani Isra'il, they marched to Palestine. The leader of the Philistines was a huge man called Jaalut (Goliath). Just looking at Jaalut terrified the Bani Isra'il.

Prophet Dawud (pbuh) was present in the army of Taalut. He was very young and had not come to fight but to attend to his three older brothers who were soldiers, and to bring news of the war back to their father. When Taalut saw that Jaalut had terrified his army, he tried to encourage his men by promising them great rewards if they faced Jaalut. He even promised that he would marry his daughter to the man who killed Jaalut.

Prophet Dawud (pbuh) went to find out what was going on. He had never fought before but went to Taalut and said: "I am fit to fight this devil because I have killed a tiger and a bear that attacked my father's sheep."

Taalut was impressed by his bravery and accepted his offer. He gave Prophet Dawud (pbuh) armour and told him to be careful.

Before Prophet Dawud (pbuh) approached Jaalut, he removed the heavy armour. He stood before the enemy, with a catapult and the staff with which he used to tend to his sheep.

Before Jaalut could react to this challenge, Prophet Dawud (pbuh) had shot a stone from his catapult. The stone struck Jaalut's forehead with terrible force and brought him to the ground in a daze. Prophet Dawud (pbuh) then drew Jaalut's heavy sword and cut off his head.

Having witnessed the death of their powerful leader, the Philistines were demoralised and ran away in panic.

Prophet Dawud (pbuh) married Taalut's daughter Mikâl. He was also made commander-in- chief of Taalut's army. After Taalut died Prophet Dawud (pbuh) became the king.

Iron was as soft as wax in his hands, and he used to make special, light-weight battle armour made of iron ringlets joined together. By selling these to the army, he earned his livelihood.

Allah blessed him with a beautiful voice and revealed the Zabur (Psalms of David) to him. When he used to recite from it, the mountains and the birds would also join in with him.

"Indeed We granted Dawud a blessing, saying, "O Mountains! sing the praise of Allah along with him, and you too, O Birds!." And We made iron soft for him."
Suratus Saba 34:10

Prophet Dawud (pbuh) ruled for many years. After him his youngest son Prophet Sulayman (pbuh) became king.

PROPHET DAWUD (PBUH)
Nineteen sons

Prophet Dawud (pbuh) had nineteen sons. Allah had granted Prophet Dawud (pbuh) the Zabur. He also became King of his people.

Each of his sons hoped to inherit their father's throne. Allah revealed to Prophet Dawud (pbuh) some questions to put to each of his sons. Whoever answered the questions correctly, would inherit his father's throne.

One day, Prophet Dawud (pbuh) called all his sons in the presence of all the scholars and leaders of all the tribes in his kingdom. He asked them all the following questions:

1) Which is the nearest thing to a human being?
2) Which is the furthest thing to a human being?
3) Which two things are attached to each other?
4) Which is the most shocking thing?
5) Which two things remain unchanged?
6) Which two things are always different?
7) Which two things are opposed to each other?
8) What is the action the result of which is good?
9) What is the action the result of which is bad?

Only the youngest son, Prophet Sulayman (pbuh) stood up and gave the following answers

1) The nearest thing to a human being is the hereafter (death may come at
2) any moment)
3) The furthest thing from a human being is the time which has passed away.
4) The two things that are attached to each other are the body and the soul.
5) The most shocking thing is a dead body (a body without a soul).
6) The two things which remain the same are the sky and the earth.
7) The two things which are different are the night and day.
8) The two things opposed to each other are life and death.
9) The action, the result of which is good is patience at the time of anger.
10) The action, the result of which is bad is haste at the time of anger.
   Prophet Sulayman (pbuh) was appointed the successor to his father's throne.

PROPHET SULAYMAN (PBUH)

He was thirteen years old when his father Prophet Dawud (pbuh) died.

Allah granted him with the greatest kingdom that any king has ever ruled over. He was also granted the blessing of knowing the language of the birds and the animals. Even the wind would obey him. His army consisted of men, jinn, animals andbirds.

He was once marching with his army to a place called the Valley of ants which had a lot of gems and valuable metals buried in it.

In the valley there were large ants which stopped people from coming into the valley.

When the chief of the ants saw the army of Prophet Sulayman (pbuh) coming, he told all the other ants to go into their holes (houses) in case Prophet Sulayman (pbuh) and his army crush them.

Prophet Sulayman (pbuh) heard what the chief of the ants had said.

Prophet Sulayman (pbuh) smiled and asked his army to be careful not to hurt the ants. Prophet Sulayman (pbuh) thanked Allah for giving him the wisdom to understand and to be able to save lives of the ants.

One day Prophet Sulayman (pbuh) noticed that his messenger bird - Hud Hud was missing. A little while later the Hud Hud came back and reported to him saying:

"...I have brought to you information from Saba (Sheba). Indeed I found a woman ruling over them and she has been given plenty and a great throne. I found her and her people worshipping the sun instead of Allah....." **Suratun Naml-27:23,24**

Prophet Sulayman (pbuh) sent a letter to Bilqis, the Queen of Saba, saying: "In the name of Allah, the Kind, the Merciful. Do not elevate yourself and come towards me in submission to Allah (as a Muslim)." **Suratun Naml 27:30,31**

When Bilqis received the letter, she consulted her ministers and decided to send Prophet Sulayman (pbuh) gifts and then wait for his reaction.

Prophet Sulayman (pbuh) welcomed the messengers and asked for the reply to his letter. When they presented him with the gifts, he said:

"What are these riches? I have been given such blessings from Allah that are matched by none.

Return to your country and inform your Queen that I am sending such an army towards Saba that no one will be able to defeat."

When Bilqis received this message and the report about the power of Prophet Sulayman (pbuh), she decided to submit herself before him and accept his invitation to embrace Islam.

When Prophet Sulayman (pbuh) learnt that she was coming to his kingdom, he turned to his people and said: "Which of you can bring me her throne before they come here in submission?" **Suratun Naml 27:38**

One jinn said: "I will bring it before you rise from your place.   "
Suratun Naml- 27:39

But one who had been taught the special name of Allah by Prophet Sulayman (pbuh) said: "Said he who had some knowledge of the Book, "I will bring it to you before your eye blinks", and when he (Sulayman) saw the throne settle beside him, he said, "This is by the Grace of my Lord so that He may test whether I am grateful or ungrateful..."
Suratun Naml - 27:40

In preparation for the arrival of Bilqis, Prophet Sulayman (pbuh) had ordered a palace of glass to be built. Under the glass floors, there was water with various kinds of fish swimming in it. When Bilqis arrived, he took her to the palace. Bilqis was fooled by the appearance of water and hitched up her dress showing her bare feet to stop it getting wet. When she realised her mistake, she at once understood what Prophet Sulayman (pbuh) was trying to tell her. He was showing her that things are not always what they seem, and even if the sun she worshipped was the most powerful thing to see, it was Allah who created it.

One day Prophet Sulayman (pbuh) called all his army of men, jinn, animals and birds together. He wanted to inspect them all. He climbed on top of his palace to see them. It was there whilst he was viewing his kingdom that the angel of death came. Prophet Sulayman (pbuh) was still leaning on his staff (stick). It was only when a worm ate through the stick and he fell that the men and jinn in his army realized that he had died.

PROPHET SULAYMAN (PBUH)
"O Sulayman! At this moment of time, I am better than you"

As Prophet Sulayman (pbuh) was walking through the valley of the ants, the chief of the ants warned his fellow ants of the coming of the army, advising them to go into their homes to avoid being crushed.

When Prophet Sulayman (pbuh) heard the warning of the chief of ants, he smiled and walked up to him, gently lifting him on the palm of hishand.

"Don't you know that I am the Prophet of Allah and that I would not harm any of Allah's creatures?" Sulayman asked the chief ant.

"Of course I do!" Said the chief "But, I feared that if my fellow ants would see the grandeur of your army, they would underestimate the grace of Allah which they receive and may become ungrateful."

The chief ant then asked Prophet Sulayman (pbuh) "May I ask you a question?"

"Yes!" said Prophet Sulayman (pbuh)

"Who is better at this moment in time?" asked the chief ant

"Why don't you answer the question yourself!" Prophet Sulayman (pbuh) said.

The chief ant replied:" At this moment in time, I am better than you for I am standing on the palm of a Prophet of Allah, whilst you O Prophet! are standing on the ground!"

PROPHET ZAKARIYYA (PBUH) & PROPHET YAHYA (PBUH)

Zakariyya (pbuh) and his wife were very old, and to their sorrow they did not have any children. They wanted very much to have a son, so Zakariyya (pbuh) prayed to Allah: Let my wife and I have a son before we die.

As Zakariyya (pbuh) was saying his prayer, an angel of Allah appeared. You have prayed to Allah and Allah has heard your prayer, the angel told him. Your wife will have a son and his name will be Yahya (pbuh). He will be a good and honourable man and he will be Allah's prophet.

Even though Zakariyya (pbuh) had prayed for this, he was surprised: But my wife and I are very old! He said. How can we have a son?

When Allah has willed a thing, it will happen, the angel assured him. As a sign that you are going to have a son, you must not speak to anyone for three days.

So it happened that even when Zakariyya (pbuh) wanted to speak to someone, he could not move his tongue. Only after three days was he able to speak again. He knew then that they were going to have a son. Both he and his wife were very happy. They prayed to Allah and thanked Him, and when the son was born, they named him Yahya (pbuh).

Yahya (pbuh) was a good and loving son. He prayed to Allah together with his father Zakariyya (pbuh) and his mother. The three of them always did good deeds. Yahya (pbuh) was very kind and good to all people and all animals. He was never proud or bad-tempered, and Allah made him His prophet. Yahya (pbuh) was a pious and humble servant of Allah and he always told people to pray to Allah because Allah had created mankind.

Allah's blessing for Yahya (pbuh) can be found in the Qur'an: "Peace was with him on the day he was born and on the day he died, and peace will be with him on the day when he will come to life again."
Whoever is as good and pious as Prophet Yahya (pbuh) will be blessed with everlasting peace by Allah.

PROPHET ISA (PBUH) (JESUS)

Imran was a good man. His wife Hanna prayed to Allah to grant her a child whom she would dedicate to the mosque in Baytul Muqaddas. Allah granted her duas and when she delivered Sayyida Maryam (pbuh), she handed her over to the mosque where she was looked after by Prophet Zakariyya (pbuh).

Prophet Zakariyya (pbuh) built her a special room where she lived. Whenever he went to visit her he found that she always had food. Prophet Zakariyya (pbuh) asked her where the food came from and she said that it came fromAllah.

One day while she was busy in her ibada, Sayyida Maryam (pbuh) was startled to see a young man suddenly appear before her. She was scared but the man said, "Do not be frightened, I am the angel Jibrail and have brought to you the glad news that Allah is soon going to bless you with a son. He will be great in this world and in the hereafter and will speak while still in his cradle." Sayyida Maryam asked, "How can this be possible when no man has ever touched me?" Jibrail said, "Allah has Power over all things."

When she felt the pangs of child birth, she was frightened. The Qur'an says:
"Then (a voice) called out to her from beneath her, "Do not grieve, your Lord has caused a stream (to flow) from beneath you. And shake towards you the trunk of the palm-tree, it will drop on you fresh ripe dates. Then eat and drink......." **Suratu Maryam, 19: 24 - 26**

She returned to Baytul Muqaddas with her baby in her arms. The Jews who saw her were surprised and began to accuse her saying that she had acted in a shameful manner while her parents had not been immoral people. She did not reply, but merely pointed at her baby.

The people of the town looked at her with suspicion. The Qur'an says:
"But she pointed unto him. They said, "How can we speak to one who is a child in the cradle?" He (Isa) said, "Verily I am a servant of Allah. He has given me a Book and made me a Prophet. And He has made me blessed wherever I am and He has enjoined on me prayer and Zakaa for as long as I live. And (to be) dutiful to my mother and He has not made me insolent
..." **Suratu Maryam 19: 29 – 31**

The miracle of Prophet Isa (pbuh) speaking to them from his cradle silenced them. The fame of the baby grew and many came from all over the country to see him. The emperor, Herodotus, learnt about the birth of Prophet Isa (pbuh) and was immediately concerned about the threat to his power. And he plotted to kill Prophet Isa (pbuh). However, Sayyida Maryam (pbuh) learnt of the danger to her son and she left with him for Egypt.

In Egypt, Prophet Isa (pbuh) lived with his mother until he was 30 years old.

The Injeel was revealed to him and he returned to Baytul Muqaddas. He was granted the miracles of curing the sick and raising the dead tolife.

From amongst the few who believed, Prophet Isa (pbuh) selected twelve as his disciples or 'hawwariyyun'. These men learnt directly from Prophet Isa (pbuh) and he gave them authority to preach to the people according to the laws laid down in the Injeel. Prophet Isa (pbuh) and his twelve disciples went from place to place, in towns and villages, inviting people to believe in One God and teaching them the Divine commandments contained in the Injeel.

The activities of Prophet Isa (pbuh) caused commotion amongst the Jews, who felt that their own religion was being threatened. They were angry that his laws were different from those laid down in the Tawrat and that he did not consider Saturday as a holy day. They accused him of causing disruptions in their community with his magic. They refused to recognise him as a Messenger of Allah just like Prophet Musa (pbuh). They finally decided to kill Prophet Isa (pbuh) and set about trying to find him. They caught one of his disciples called Yahuda (Judas) who betrayed Prophet Isa (pbuh) for thirty pieces of silver.

The Jews had decided to arrest Prophet Isa (pbuh) and crucify him by nailing his hands and feet onto a wooden cross. Prophet Isa (pbuh) heard that the Jews planned to arrest him and he took shelter in a vacant house. Yahuda knew this and he led the Jews to the house.

Allah raised him to the heavens.

Meanwhile, Yahuda entered the house but found it empty. Allah caused Yahuda to resemble Prophet Isa (pbuh). When he came out of the house, they seized him and dragged him away. Despite his protests, he was crucified. The Jews and even the Christians thus say that Prophet Isa (pbuh) was killed on the cross but the Qur'ansays:

وَقُل رَّبِّ زِدْنِي عِلْمًا

"That they said (boastfully), "Verily we killed the Messiah, Isa son of Mary, the Apostle of God."; but they killed him not, nor crucified him, but it was made to appear to them (that they had). And those who differ therein are full of doubts, with no (certain) knowledge. They only pursue a conjecture. They certainly did not kill him. Nay, Allah raised (lifted) him up to Himself; and Allah isMighty, Wise". **Suratun Nisa, 4: 157,158**

When the 12th Holy Imam (pbuh) will re-appear, Prophet Isa (pbuh) will descend from the heavens and offer prayers behind him. The Christian Era (A.D.) dates from the death of Prophet Isa (pbuh). He was 33 years old when he was raised to the heavens.

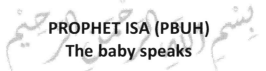

PROPHET ISA (PBUH)
The baby speaks

Imran was a good man. His wife was called Hanna.

Hanna made a promise to Allah that she would give her baby to serve Allah. She asked Allah to keep her baby safe from Shaytan. When her baby was born she called her Maryam.

Hanna kept her promise and took baby Maryam to the temple in Jerusalem. Here Sayyida Maryam was looked after by Prophet Zakariyya (pbuh) who was her uncle.

One day when she was a young lady, the angel Jibrail came to her room and told her that she was to have a baby whose name would be Isa – son of Maryam. He told her that he would be a Prophet of Allah and would speak even when he was a baby in the cradle.

Sayyida Maryam was surprised. She asked the angel how she could have a baby without a husband. The angel told her that Allah could do whatever He wished.

After Prophet Isa (pbuh) was born, Sayyida Maryam was worried as to how she would tell the people of the town about him. She was ordered by Allah to keep silent and let baby Isa talk.

When the people of the town asked her about the baby, she pointed to him
"I am a servant of Allah; He has given me the book (Injeel) and made me a Prophet."
Qur'an – Suratu Maryam 19:30

The book that Allah gave him is called the Injeel.

He grew up to teach the people about Allah telling them that there were no gods except Allah.

He was given the miracle of curing the sick and making dead people come back to life.

PROPHET ISA (PBUH)
Up to heaven!

The enemies of Prophet Isa (pbuh) wanted to get rid of him. They did not like him talking about Allah and asking people to be good Muslims.

They made a plan to kill him. When Prophet Isa (pbuh) found out about their plan he went to live away in a secret hideout which only his close companions knew of.

The enemies gave 30 pieces of silver to one of the companions of Prophet Isa (pbuh) to tell them where he was. When the enemy soldiers came to the hideout to arrest him, Allah had raised him up to heaven.

The soldiers did not find anyone but Allah had changed the face of the companion who had given away the secret to look like that of Prophet Isa (pbuh)

The soldiers arrested him and nailed him to a cross thinking it was Prophet Isa (pbuh) Allah saved His Prophet.

Prophet Isa (pbuh) is still alive in the heavens and will come back to earth when Imam Muhammad Al-Mahdi (pbuh) reappears.

PROPHET MUHAMMAD (PBUH)
Hazrat Abdullah (pbuh) & Sayyida Amina (pbuh)

The Christian priests had a shirt that belonged to Prophet Yahya (pbuh). They knew from their scriptures that when the father of the last Prophet would be born, blood would appear on the shirt.

They knew therefore when Hazrat Abdullah (pbuh) was born and were searching for him. He was his father's favourite son.

Abdul Muttalib had vowed that when he had ten sons he would sacrifice one. He drew lots and the name of Abdullah came up. Abdullah was very good and much liked by the people of Makka. When they saw that Abdul Muttalib was going to sacrifice him they persuaded him to go to a wise woman in Yathrib who could tell him of an alternative sacrifice.

It was agreed that lots would be drawn using camels. 10 lots were drawn of 10 camels each. Eventually 100 camels were sacrificed and Abdullah was saved.
The Prophet (Pbuh) used to say that he was the son of two sacrifices - Ismail & Abdullah.

Abdul Muttalib dreamt that Abdullah should be married to Amina daughter of Wahab. They were married a year before the 'Year of the Elephant'.

When Sayyida Amina (pbuh) was pregnant, Abdullah went with a trade caravan to Syria. On the way back he fell ill and died before the Prophet (pbuh) was born. He is buried in Madina.

He left some camels, goats and a slave girl called Umme Ayman which were given to the Prophet (pbuh)

Sayyida Amina was very sad after her husband died. When the Prophet (pbuh) was six years old she too died on the way back from visiting Abdullah's grave. She is buried in Abwa, a place between Makka and Madina.

BIRTH OF PROPHET MUHAMMAD (PBUH)

Imam Ja'fer As-Sadiq (pbuh) has said that Allah created the light of Prophet Muhammad (Pbuh) before any of his creations.

He was born in the year of the Elephant (570 C.E.) in the month of Rabi ul Awwal.
It was just after sunrise on Friday the seventeenth.

Shaytan who had been previously allowed to visit the heavens suddenly found that he could not go. He went to the Ka'ba disguised as a little bird and saw angels celebrating. Jibrail saw him and recognised him. He was asked to leave but asked Jibrail to tell him what had happened. Jibrail told him that the last of the Prophets; Muhammad (pbuh) was born.
Shaytan left weeping and wailing. It is said that he wept for forty days.

It is also said that all the idols fell on their faces and the palace of Kisra who was emperor of Persia started shaking and had cracks in it.

Abdul Muttalib saw a white cloud shadowing the house of Sayyida Amina (pbuh) and ran to enquire. He was told of the birth of Muhammad(pbuh)

Inspired by Allah, Abdul Muttalib named the child Muhammad. When asked why; he replied that he wished that Muhammad should be praised in the heavens and in the earth (Muhammad means one who is praiseworthy).

It is said that Sayyida Amina (pbuh) had named him Ahmed before Abdul Muttalib called him Muhammad.

PROPHET MUHAMMAD (PBUH)

Prophet Muhammad (pbuh) was looked after by his grandfather Abdul Muttalib and his uncle Abu Talib because his father had died before he was born.

When he grew up he got married to Sayyida Khadija (pbuh) she was a very good lady who gave all her money for Islam. They had a daughter called Sayyida Fatima Zahra (pbuh)

The people of Makka used to believe in many gods which they made out of wood, flour, stones and other things. They kept them in the Ka'ba. Prophet Muhammad (pbuh) told the people of Makka that there is no God except Allah and that he Muhammad was the messenger of Allah.

Allah sent him messages through the angel Jibrail. One message is called an aya. The messages are the ayaat of the Qur'an.

The Makkans did not like Prophet Muhammad (pbuh) and wanted to kill him so he left Makka and went to Madina. This journey of his is called Hijra from which date the Muslim calendar begins. Most of the people of Madina became good Muslims.

As ordered to him by Allah the Prophet (pbuh) chose Imam Ali (pbuh) to be the leader after him at a place called Ghadeer. At Ghadeer the Prophet (pbuh) also told the Muslims that he would soon be returning to Allah and that after him they should follow the Qur'an and his Ahlulbayt.

He died on the 28th of Safar in Madina when he was 63 years old.

AL – AMIN
(The trustworthy one)

Once, the Ka'ba was being rebuilt. The people of Makka were all working together to build it.

When the walls reached the level where they had to place the 'Hajar al-Aswad' (The black stone) the work stopped. Everyone wanted to place the black stone in its position because it was so important.

There was a big argument and it seemed like there would be a civil war in Makka. A wise man spoke out and said:

"Do not make war because it destroys homes and cities. It causes misery and hardship. Find a solution to your problem."

He suggested that they choose a person who would decide what to do from themselves. The people asked who and how they should choose. The wise man suggested that they appoint the first person who enters Masjid al-Haram through a particular door which he pointed towards.

Everyone agreed and all eyes were fixed on the door.

A young man entered. Everyone was glad for it was Muhammad Al-Amin (Pbuh) (The Trustworthy One). They crowded around him and told him what had happened.

He told them:

"All the leading men of Makka must share in this important work." The people looked surprised:

"How is that possible?"

Muhammad (Pbuh) gave instructions for all the leaders of the tribes to be present. When they had all assembled he took off his cloak and placed the Hajar al-Aswad in the middle. He asked all the leaders to pick the cloak and bring it to the side of the Ka'ba.

Muhammad (Pbuh) gently guided the stone to its special place. All the people were pleased. He had not yet declared his prophethood but even then the people of Makka used to turn to him to settle their differences.

ANNOUNCEMENT OF PROPHETHOOD

As soon as the Prophet (pbuh) announced that there are no gods but Allah, he was rejected totally. He remained the same person - with the excellent akhlaq but what had changed is that he had declared his belief in Allah.

When he was forty he got the first revelations in the cave of Hira in mountain of Noor (Light) where he used to meditate. It was brought by angel Jibrail and it was the first five ayaat of Suratul Alaq.

"Read in the name of your Lord who created (all); He created man from a clot of blood;

Read! Your Lord is the most bountiful,

Who by the pen taught man what he did not know".

It was the 27th of Rajab (The day of Be'that) in the 14th year of the life of the Prophet. He was busy in remembrance of Allah in his usual place in the cave of Mount Noor (a mountain situated in the north of Makka). The angel Jibrail came to him and recited to him the above ayaat of the Qur'an. The Prophet had not been taught to read and write by any on earth but his abilities were taught to him by the Lord.

The first person who the Prophet told of this was his wife - Sayyida Khadija. She immediately testified to his Prophethood and gave him her fullsupport.

The Prophet began the preaching of his mission to a limited circle for the first three years. Then he was asked by Allah to invite his near relationsto Islam.

"And warn yournearest relatives." **Suratush Shu'ara 26:214**

The Prophet (pbuh) arranged a meal inviting 40 of his relations. This is known as 'Da'watul Dhul Ashira'. He invited them towards Allah and introduced himself as the Messenger of Allah. He then asked thrice:

"Which one of you will support me so that he may become my brother, wasi and successor after me?"

Each time Imam Ali (pbuh) who was 15 years old at the time stood up and said: "O Prophet of Allah! I am prepared to supportyou!"

The Prophet (pbuh) held Imam Ali's (pbuh) hand high and told his audience that Ali (pbuh) would be his successor and they should listen to him and follow him. The others who were present taunted Abu Talib saying he would now have to take orders from his son. The meeting ended.

After this he began preaching openly to the Quraysh who reacted violently. The Prophet and his followers were constantly harassed. The Prophet was not allowed to worship in the Ka'ba. Thorns were strewn in his path, dirt and filth were thrown at him, he was accused of being a madman, magician and poet and was taunted and insulted. His faithful companions too were tortured. Some were placed on the hot sands and heavy stones were put on their chests, nooses were put round their necks and they were dragged in the streets. The first martyr of Islam was Sumayya, the mother of one of the companions of the Prophet, Ammar Yasir.

The Prophet had about 100 followers and physical cruelty made life unbearable in Makka. The Prophet advised his followers to got to Abyssinia under the leadership of Jaffer Tayyar. This was the first Hijra in Islam (in the fifth year of Prophet hood) and 15 people took part in it. The Prophet then advised a second Hijra.

When the Quraysh found out that the Muslims were living peacefully in Abyssinia, they sent expensive gifts to the ministers of the King of Abyssinia to bribe them. Then they sent their representative Amr Al-Aas who visited King Najashi (of Abyssinia) asking for the return of the Muslims claiming that they had invented a new religion. The ministers loudly supported the request.

King Najashi asked whether the Muslims had killed anyone, stolen property or committed any crimes. Amr relied that their only crime was the invention of a new religion. King Najashi called Ja'fer bin Abu Talib to the court and asked him why the Muslims had abandoned the religion of their forefathers and started a new religion. King Najashi was impressed with what Ja'fer said and asked him to recite some ayaat from the Qur'an. Ja'fer recited ayaat from Suratu Maryam which moved the King and his ministers. Frustrated that they could not overcome the Prophet, the Quraysh boycotted the families of Hashim and Muttalib, having no contact with them nor allowing food or drink to reach to them. Abu Talib had no choice but to take them to a valley belonging to him called Shib-e-Abu Talib.

For three long years from Muharram in the 7th year after declaration of Prophethood they stayed there under so much hardship that at times they lived on leaves and grass. They came out when the Prophet told Abu Talib that the agreement signed by all the Quraysh to boycott them had been eaten up by insects and only the words "In the name of our Lord..." remained. Abu Talib went and told this to the Quraysh who found it to be true and had no choice but to stop their boycott.

Shortly after Abu Talib and Khadija both died and this grieved the Prophet so much that he called the year Aamul Huzn (The year of grief).

PROPHET MUHAMMAD (PBUH)

"The hour drew near and the moon was split apart; and if they see a miracle they turn aside and say: It ismagic! ..." **Suratul Qamar - 54:2,3**

The people of Makka once came to the Prophet (pbuh) and said: "If you are a Prophet of Allah, then make the moon split into two!"

The Prophet (pbuh) pointed to the moon and with Allah's help the moon was seen split into two parts.

A man called Ibn Abbas says that he saw the peak of Mount Hira between the two parts of the moon.

The people then asked for the two parts to be joined together and it was done.

They saw the miracle with their own eyes. The Jews who were present became Muslims but the Makkans like Abu Jahl said it was magic and walkedaway.

The crack is present in the moon even today.

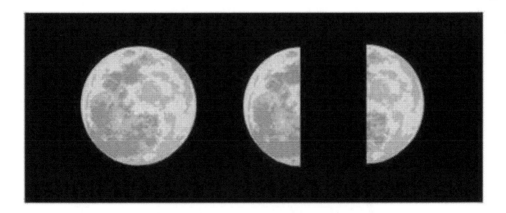

PROPHET MUHAMMAD (PBUH)
Me'raj

One night the angel Jibrail came to Prophet Muhammad (pbuh) and said that he was to go on a special journey.

The Prophet (pbuh) rode on a special animal called Buraq which travelled faster than lightning. In Arabic lightning is Barq.

Prophet Muhammad (pbuh) was taken from the Ka'ba to Madina where he was later to go. From there he was taken to Mount Sinai where Prophet Musa (pbuh) had an appointment with Allah for forty nights.

From there he went to Baytulhaam (Bethlehem) where Prophet Isa (pbuh) was born and then to Baytul Muqaddas (Jerusalem) where in the mosque of Aqsa he led Salatul Jama'a praying with all the other Prophets sent before him.

From Baytul Muqaddas, Buraq took him to the heavens where he met all the other Prophets and saw the places of punishment and the places of blessings.

He also went to the masjid in the heavens.

Allah says in the Qur'an that the Prophet (pbuh) was taken on this special journey so he could see some of the wonderful signs of Allah.

When we have a very good friend we too want to show them our secrets and treasures. Prophet Muhammad (pbuh) is a perfect Muslim who obeyed Allah all the time and so is very close to Allah.

بسم الله الرحمن الرحيم

PROPHET MUHAMMAD (PBUH)
Hijra to Madina

The people of Makka who did not believe in Allah had tried everything. They tried to stop the Prophet (pbuh) from believing in Allah by offering him riches and comfort but that did not work. They tried to be nasty to him and his followers but that too did not work so they decided to kill him. They chose one person from each tribe to meet one night and kill the Prophet (pbuh) whilst he was sleeping.

Allah had told the Prophet (pbuh) of their plan through the angel Jibrail. The Prophet (pbuh) asked Imam Ali (pbuh) to sleep in his bed that night. On hearing the request Imam Ali (pbuh) immediately did a sijda of shukr to thank Allah for having given him the honour of protecting the Prophet (pbuh).

The Prophet (pbuh) recited some ayaat of Suratu Yaseen and slipped out of the house under the very noses of the killers. Imam Ali (pbuh) had never slept more peacefully.

Later in the night, the killers burst into the house. They lifted the blanket to find Imam Ali (pbuh) sleeping in the Prophet's (pbuh) place.

Their plan had failed.

Prophet Muhammad (pbuh) was on his way to Madina where the people had invited him to come.

وقل رب زدني علماً

FAREWELL HAJJ

Since the time when Prophet Ibrahim (pbuh) had built the Holy Ka'ba, it had been a place of worship. Over the years, this worship had deteriorated into strange and undesirable practices. People used to dance naked around the Holy Ka'ba, and they had put idols inside it.

Even after the conquest of Mecca when these idols were broken, the people did not know how to perform the Hajj ceremonies properly. The Prophet (pbuh) therefore performed Hajj in 10 A.H., so that the people would remain in no doubt as to how it should be done.

He could also instruct the people about the boundaries of Mina and Arafaat and teach them about the times of departure from these places.

In Dhulqa'da he announced that he was going to perform the Hajj that year. Thousands gathered outside Madina awaiting the departure of the Prophet (Pbuh).

The Prophet (Pbuh) appointed Abu Dajana as his representative in Madina and proceeded toward Makka taking with him 60 animals for sacrifice.

At Zil Hulayfa, in the mosque of Shajara, he put on his Ihram.

At Arafat, the Prophet (pbuh) whilst mounted on his camel, delivered his famous and historical speech to the thousands of people who had gathered. He addressed the people and went through a summary of his teachings to them. He repeated all the major and minor elements of Islamic principles so that there could be no doubt left in their minds. When he finished he offered his noon and afternoon prayers with 100,000 men.

The Prophet (pbuh) then completed the Hajj

This Hajj is known as Hajjatul Wida (the Farewell Hajj) because it was the last Hajj that the Prophet (Pbuh) performed in his life.

During this Hajj he demonstrated every feature of the ceremony, so that there could be no confusion later.

A VERY SPECIAL ANNOUNCEMENT

It was a hot sunny day. Lots and lots of people were coming back from Makka after doing hajj with the Prophet (pbuh). They stopped at a place near Johfa which was known as Ghadeer e Khum.

The angel Jibraail came and told the Prophet (pbuh) that he had a special announcement for the Prophet (Pbuh) to make to the people.

The Prophet (pbuh) asked Bilal to give the adhaan. Bilal had a beautiful voice and he was the Prophet's favourite muadhin (Someone who gives adhaan). When the people heard the adhan, they all came to hear the Prophet (pbuh). Even those who had gone forward came back. After the Dhuhr salaa, Prophet Muhammed (pbuh) stood on a pulpit made out of saddles.

He told the people that he was soon to die. He was leaving behind two very important things which the Muslims should always follow:
The Quran and The AhlulBayt.

He then held the hand of Imam Ali (pbuh) high up and told the people that as per the command of Allah, Imam Ali (Pbuh) would be the leader of the Muslims after him. He said:

For whosoever I am the mawla (master), Ali is his mawla (master). He repeated this three times.

As soon as he had announced this, Jibraail brought another message from Allah which said that Islam was now complete and perfect. This was the last aya of the Qur'an to be revealed. It is aya 3 of Suratul Ma'ida.

WAFAT OF PROPHET MUHAMMAD (PBUH)

In the Muharram of the year 11 A.H. Prophet Muhammad (pbuh) became very ill.

Three days before he died he asked for a paper, pen and ink so he could write some advice for the Muslims so that they would always stay on the right path.

On the 28th of Safar 11 A.H. Prophet Muhammad (pbuh) died with his head resting in the lap of Imam Ali (pbuh)

The last thing he said was:
Salaa! Salaa!!

Imam Ali (pbuh) gave him ghusl and kafan and it was he who buried him in his house which was joined to the mosque of Madina.

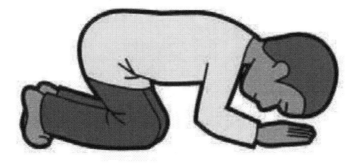